POWER
in the NAME

POWER
in the NAME

REVEALING THE GOD WHO PROVIDES AND HEALS

DEREK PRINCE

WHITAKER
HOUSE

Editor's Note: This book was compiled from the extensive archive of Derek Prince's unpublished materials and edited by the Derek Prince Ministries editorial team.

POWER IN THE NAME:
Revealing the God Who Provides and Heals

ISBN: 978-1-60374-121-7
Printed in the United States of America
© 2009 by Derek Prince Ministries, International

Derek Prince Ministries
P.O. Box 19501
Charlotte, North Carolina 28219
www.derekprince.org

Whitaker House
1030 Hunt Valley Circle
New Kensington, PA 15068
www.whitakerhouse.com

Library of Congress Cataloging-in-Publication Data

Prince, Derek.
  Power in the name / by Derek Prince.
    p. cm.
  Summary: "Explores the nature and purposes of the triune God through biblical manifestations, names, titles, and roles, and emphasizes His power to meet all our needs"—Provided by publisher.
  ISBN 978-1-60374-121-7 (trade pbk. : alk. paper) 1. God (Christianity)—Name. I. Title.
  BT180.N2P75 2009
  231—dc22
                                        2009013374

3 4 5 6 7 8 9 10 11 12 **W** 16 15 14 13 12 11 10

CONTENTS

Preface

All through the Bible, names have great significance—much greater significance than they usually have in our contemporary culture. Almost every name in the Bible has a specific meaning and a specific appropriateness to the person named; each is indicative of the nature of that person.

A clear example of this fact is found in the names of the three patriarchs, Abraham, Isaac, and Jacob. Two of them had their names changed by God—Abraham and Jacob. Abraham's name was originally Abram, meaning "exalted father," while Abraham means "father of a multitude." Jacob's name was changed to Israel; Jacob is usually interpreted as "supplanter," while Israel means either "a prince with God" or "one who wrestles with God."

In each case, the change of name was given during a crisis in the life of the patriarch, and it had a decisive effect on his ongoing character development and the fulfillment of his destiny. In other words, names are connected with character and destiny.

You might ask, "Why didn't Isaac have his name changed?" Interestingly, God chose Isaac's name before he was born. Since it was chosen by God, Isaac's name did not need to be changed.

If the names given to men in the Bible are of such significance, the names attributed to God must be that much more significant. In the chapters that follow, we will look at how God is revealed in His names, as well as how God "disguises" Himself and how His ultimate revelation of Himself may be found in Jesus Christ and the titles by which Jesus is called.

SECTION 1

GOD REVEALED IN HIS NAMES

Introduction to Section 1

Unity and Plurality: Father, Son, and Holy Spirit

One particular aspect of God that is absolutely unique to the Bible's revelation of God—it is not found in any other book or religion—is the combination of unity and plurality within God's nature. This unique aspect is revealed in His name *Elohim*, a name we will study in more detail in chapter 1. Significantly, this name occurs in the first verse of the Bible. In Genesis 1:1, we find these words:

In the beginning God created the heavens and the earth.

In the original Hebrew, there is a kind of clash of grammar in this verse. The noun "*God*," *Elohim*, is plural, yet the verb that follows, "*created*," is singular. So, we have a plural noun followed by a singular verb. This paradox contains the seeds of truth that are unfolded throughout the rest of Scripture.

There is a somewhat similar paradox in the famous verse in Deuteronomy that the Jewish people call the *Shema*, which is more or less a doctrinal statement of the faith of Israel:

Hear, O Israel! The Lord is our God, the Lord is one!"
(Deuteronomy 6:4)

Interestingly, it takes only four words to say "*The Lord is our God, the Lord is one*" in Hebrew. Still more interesting, of those four words, three are plural in form. The only word that is singular is the word for "*one*." So, again, we find this paradox of unity and plurality combined in the revelation of God.

Two Words for "One"

One way to understand unity and plurality is to realize that there are two different Hebrew words for "one." One word is *yachid* and the other is *echad*.

Yachid: Alone and Unique

The word *yachid* means "that which is absolutely alone and unique." For instance, in Genesis 22:2, the Lord said to Abraham, "*Take now your son, your only son, whom you love....*" This verse uses the word "*only*," yachid, because Abraham and Sarah had only one son born of their own bodies.

Another example is in Psalm 25:16, where the psalmist wrote, "*I am lonely and afflicted.*" The word "*lonely*" is *yachid*, meaning "entirely on my own."

Echad: A Union of a Number of Elements

On the other hand, the other word for "one," *echad*, denotes a union of a number of elements. This meaning is very clear in many passages of the Old Testament. For instance, in Genesis 2, Scripture outlines the nature of marriage and the union of Adam and Eve:

> *For this cause a man shall leave his father and his mother, and shall cleave to his wife; and they shall become one flesh.*
> (Genesis 2:24)

The word "*one*," *echad*, expresses that the two are being united to become one. So, *echad* describes or denotes the union of more than one to form a unity.

In Numbers 13, the Scripture says this of the Israelite spies who went in to see the Promised Land:

Then they came to the valley of Eshcol and from there cut down a branch with a single cluster of grapes. (Numbers 13:23)

The word "*single*" in Hebrew is *echad*. It was one cluster, but it was made up of many grapes.

We find this word used again in a remarkable statement in the book of Judges, when there was civil war among the tribes of Israel:

Thus all the men of Israel were gathered against the city, united as one man. (Judges 20:11)

The word "*one*" here is *echad*. There were many thousands of men; nevertheless, they formed a unity.

In one of the prophet Ezekiel's visions, the Lord told him to take two sticks and to name them for the two leading tribes of Israel.

And you, son of man, take for yourself one stick and write on it, "For Judah and for the sons of Israel, his companions"; then take another stick and write on it, "For Joseph, the stick of Ephraim and all the house of Israel, his companions." Then join them for yourself one to another into one stick, that they may become one in your hand. (Ezekiel 37:16–17)

Again, the word "*one*" is *echad*, yet we see specifically that there were originally two sticks. In being united, they formed a unity, which is described by the word "*one*."

Unity That Is a Union

I believe these examples help us to understand the kind of unity that is represented by the word *Elohim*. It is a unity that is a union—a perfect union—but contains more than oneness: plurality.

Let us review two passages in the Bible where this understanding is clear. In Genesis 3, after Adam and Eve had sinned and forfeited their right to live in the garden of Eden, we read,

> *Then the LORD God said, "Behold, the man has become like one of Us, knowing good and evil."*   (Genesis 3:22)

In reading the whole of Genesis 3, it is clear that having the knowledge of good and evil was a distinctive characteristic of God. In the *New American Standard Bible*, the word "*Us*" in verse 22 is capitalized. In other words, it applies to God. There is both unity and plurality within the very nature of God.

Another interesting example is in Isaiah's description of his vision of the Lord:

> *Then I heard the voice of the Lord, saying, "Whom shall I send, and who will go for Us?" Then I said, "Here am I. Send me!"*
>   (Isaiah 6:8)

God was speaking, and He used both the singular ("*I*") and the plural ("*Us*"). He said, "*Whom shall I send, and who will go for Us?*"

The Three in One

All through the Bible, there is this fascinating paradox: God is one; yet, within the oneness of God, there is more than one. The full truth of this paradox of the unity and the plurality of God is brought to light and into open revelation in the New Testament.

Let us look at the most distinctive of many such passages, the final commission of Jesus to His disciples as recorded at the end of Matthew's gospel:

> *Go therefore and make disciples of all the nations, baptizing them in the name of the Father and the Son and the Holy Spirit.*
>   (Matthew 28:19)

Actually, the Greek says, "Baptizing them *into* the name of the Father and the Son and the Holy Spirit." We are to be baptized into the name of God. That act signifies taking up our places in God, losing our personal lives in God.

The fullness of God consists of the Father, the Son, and the Holy Spirit. When we see this, we understand why, right from the beginning of the Bible, in the very first verse of the Old Testament, the word for God is plural in form. The truth brought out in the New Testament is not new—it is merely an unfolding and a fulfillment of what was already present, by implication, in the Old Testament.

The fullness of God consists of the Father, the Son, and the Holy Spirit.

Let's look at two additional examples from the Old Testament. In Proverbs 30:4, the writer said,

> *Who has gone up to heaven and come down? Who has gathered up the wind in the hollow of his hands? Who has wrapped up the waters in his cloak? Who has established all the ends of the earth? What is his name, and the name of his son? Tell me if you know!* (Proverbs 30:4 NIV)

Anyone who is familiar with the revelation of Scripture will understand that the "*who*" being referred to here is God Himself. No one but God has done those things. Yet it says, "*What is his name, and the name of his son?*" This verse is part of the Old Testament's revelation of the plurality of God—in this instance, revealing the truth of, and the relationship between, God the Father and God the Son.

Then, in Isaiah 48:12–13, we read,

> *Listen to Me, O Jacob, even Israel whom I called; I am He, I am the first, I am also the last. Surely My hand founded the earth,*

*and My right hand spread out the heavens; when I call to them,
they stand together.*

Again, the whole revelation of Scripture would agree that the
person who says these words is no less than God Himself—the first
and the last, the Creator and the sustainer of heaven and earth.
Then, He says,

> *Come near to Me, listen to this: from the first I have not
> spoken in secret, from the time it took place, I was there.
> And now the Lord GOD has sent Me, and His Spirit.*
> (Isaiah 48:16)

The King James Version says, "*The Lord God, and his Spirit,
hath sent me.*" Here, a divine Person is speaking, and yet He says
that God, and His Spirit, "*has sent Me.*" Whichever way you look
at it, the fulfillment is found in the New Testament: God the Father
sent Jesus and the Holy Spirit. Both proceeded from God. And all
three are God: the Father, the Son, and the Holy Spirit. So, we see
that in *Elohim*, there is a perfect unity that is more than one. God is
essentially one, and essentially more than one. That is the mystery of
the nature of God—this unique blending of unity and plurality.

1

Elohim

The First Great Hebrew Name of God

The primary name for God in Old Testament Hebrew is *Elohim*, the name we looked at in the introduction in relation to the unity and plurality of God. Let's return to Genesis 1:1, where we find these words:

In the beginning God [Elohim] created the heavens and the earth.

Thereafter, the same name, *Elohim*, occurs about 2,500 times in the Old Testament. The Bible is a God-centered book for God-hungry humanity. Somewhere deep inside every human being, there is a hunger to know the truth about God. The Bible is the only book that can truly satisfy this hunger. That is the reason for its continuing appeal to the human race. It remains the unchallenged best seller among all books ever written.

The True God

We have seen that one very important fact about the word *Elohim* is that it is plural in form. The ending *im* is the normal plural ending in Hebrew. Just as we put an "s" at the end of many singular nouns in English to make them plural, so in Hebrew they put *im* on the end of masculine nouns to make them plural.

Interestingly, there is a singular form of that word, *Eloah*, which occurs more than fifty times in the Bible, mainly in the book of Job. The book of Job is quite possibly the oldest book in the Bible, so this indicates that *Eloah* is an older form of the word that gradually went out of use.

Another fascinating fact about *Elohim* is that even though it is plural in form, it is usually followed by a singular verb. In the Hebrew language, as in many other languages, verbs have both singular and plural forms. As we noted earlier, in Genesis 1:1, "*In the beginning God created...,*" the noun "*God*" is plural, while the verb "*created*" is in the singular form.

Though the verb that follows *Elohim* is normally singular in the Bible, there are some very interesting places where it is followed by a plural verb. One of the most interesting is in Genesis 20:13, where Abraham said, "*God [Elohim] caused me to wander from my father's house.*" The verb phrase used there, "*caused me to wander,*" is plural. There is no question that Abraham was talking about the true God who appeared to him and prompted him to leave.

Significantly, when Abraham made this statement, he was talking to a Gentile king. It occurs to me that perhaps he may have adapted his language a little bit to correspond to the mind-set of the king. As we have seen, there is an interesting balance between the singular and the plural that starts right away as soon as the name of God is mentioned in the Bible.

Eternal Power and Divine Nature

Let's talk a little more about the form *Elohim*. Both *Eloah* and *Elohim* (singular and plural forms) are derived from an earlier word, *El*, meaning "power." It is used, for instance, with that meaning in Genesis 31. Jacob and his father-in-law, Laban, have had a disagreement, and Laban says to Jacob, "*It is in my power to do you harm*" (verse 29). This statement may be translated more literally, "It is in

the power of my hand to do you harm."
The word "*power*" is *el*, the same word that
is used for God.

The basic connotation or association of
those three words—*El, Eloah, Elohim*—
stems from the one root form *el*. Their basic
meaning is "the powerful one." The plural
Elohim suggests the totality of all that is
God. This concept was expressed by the
apostle Paul in the New Testament:

The plural Elohim suggests the totality of all that is God.

> *For since the creation of the world God's invisible qualities—*
> *his eternal power and divine nature—have been clearly seen,*
> *being understood from what has been made, so that men are*
> *without excuse.*   (Romans 1:20 NIV)

Paul was saying that there are certain aspects of God that are
manifested in creation. He called them His "*invisible qualities.*"
Then, he defined them as "*his eternal power and divine nature.*"
That is really what *Elohim* stands for—God's eternal power and
divine nature.

It is interesting to note that the *Jerusalem Bible* uses the phrase
"*power and deity*" in translating the above verse. Perhaps, in a way, the
most comprehensive way to translate *Elohim* is "deity," because we have
to take into account its plural form. It really sums up all that is God.

Other Applications of Elohim

The word *elohim* is also applied in the Bible to persons other
than the one true God, but it is always for some specific reason. It is
used for persons or created things that, in some measure, manifest
one or more attributes associated with God as *Elohim*—particularly, the attributes of power, majesty, and authority. For instance, the
psalmist wrote,

> *For thou hast made him a little lower than the angels
> [elohim], and hast crowned him with glory and honour.*
> (Psalm 8:5 KJV)

This verse is usually interpreted as a prophetic preview of the incarnation of Jesus as a man. Yet it says, "*Thou hast made him a little lower than the angels.*" Other translations use "*heavenly beings*" (NIV) and "God" (NASB), so there is a good deal of flexibility. But it is generally agreed that the meaning there is angels, so we see the word *elohim* applied to angels.

The word is also applied to human judges. In Exodus 22:9, the law of Moses says this:

> *For every breach of trust, whether it is for ox, for donkey, for sheep, for clothing, or for any lost thing about which one says, "This is it," the case of both parties shall come before the judges [elohim]; he whom the judges [elohim] condemn shall pay double to his neighbor.*

The name *elohim* is conferred on human judges because they represent God's justice.

Elohim is applied to rulers in Psalm 82:1:

> *God takes His stand in His own congregation; He judges in the midst of the rulers [elohim].*

Finally, in Exodus 12:12, the word is applied to satanic principalities and powers. God said,

> *For I will go through the land of Egypt on that night, and will strike down all the first-born in the land of Egypt, both man and beast; and against all the gods [elohim] of Egypt I will execute judgments—I am the LORD.*

In this case, these "*gods*" are the enemies of the true God and His people. They are undoubtedly Satan's principalities and powers—the rulers in his satanic kingdom—but they are called gods.

So, we see that the word *elohim* is applied to angels, human judges, human rulers, and even demonic beings. That is because they all, to a limited degree, manifest one or more attributes associated with God—such as power, majesty, righteousness, justice, eternity, heavenly being—and God's attributes are summed up, I believe, in one word: *deity*.

The Full Meaning of Elohim

In the Introduction, we saw that the word *Elohim* contains within it the seed of a truth that is unfolded throughout the rest of the Bible. The essence of this truth can be stated in a paradox: *Elohim* represents the perfect unity of that which is more than one. God is essentially one and essentially more than one. The ongoing development of this paradox through the Scriptures eventually leads to the full revelation of God given by Jesus, who identified the plurality within the unity of God as Father, Son, and Spirit. A proper understanding of *Elohim* enables us to see that the revelation of Jesus is not a departure from the original revelation of the Old Testament but rather its logical fulfillment.

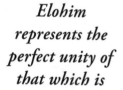

Elohim represents the perfect unity of that which is more than one.

Then, in this chapter, we have seen that the basic meaning of God's name *Elohim* is "the powerful one," and that its plural form suggests the totality of all that is God in His eternal power and divine nature.

2

Jehovah, or Yahweh

The Second Great Hebrew Name of God

We will now examine the second great Hebrew name of God, which has traditionally been represented in English by the word *Jehovah*. *Jehovah* is not the only word used for this name in English, however. In the *Jerusalem Bible*, it is written *Yahweh*. This probably represents something close to the original pronunciation in Hebrew. In another version, the *Berkeley Bible*, this name is translated "*The Eternal.*" In other words, it is translated by an adjective. We see that there is a certain mystery that revolves around this name.

Y-H-W-H

In its original Hebrew form, this name consists of four consonants, Y–H–W–H, and no vowels. We need to understand that, normally, in the Hebrew language, only the consonants are written. The vowels have to be supplied by the reader. Sometimes, they are placed under the consonants. In any case, here is the basic principle: unless you already know a word, you usually cannot pronounce it because you do not know where to place the vowels or what vowels to insert.

There are four consonants in this sacred, unique name of God. Since the time of the second temple of Israel, this name has not been pronounced by the Jewish people. It was considered too sacred for them to pronounce. So, wherever this name occurs in the Hebrew Scriptures, they substituted another name. Usually, they substituted *Adonai*, which means "my Lord." *Adon* means "Lord." (The interesting fact is that the word *Adonai*, like *Elohim*, is plural in form; the singular form is *Adoni*.) Alternatively, instead of pronouncing this name, Jewish people will simply say, "The Name."

Since this second name of God is revealed in Scripture as just four consonants, if we are going to pronounce it, we have to determine what vowels to put in. In most English versions of the Bible, this name is represented by the words "*the* LORD," where "LORD" is set in small capital letters. Many people read the Bible without realizing this. If the word "*Lord*" is not in capitals, then it represents the use of *Adon* in the original Hebrew text. But if the word "LORD" is in small capital letters, it represents the sacred name of Jehovah: *Y-H-W-H*.

Let's look at the explanation of this name that the Lord Himself gave. The Lord had told Moses he was to go back to Egypt and deliver Israel, and Moses asked,

> "*Suppose I go to the Israelites and say to them, 'The God [Elohim] of your fathers has sent me to you,' and they ask me, 'What is his name?' Then what shall I tell them?" God said to Moses, "I AM WHO I AM. This is what you are to say to the Israelites: 'I AM has sent me to you.'" God also said to Moses, "Say to the Israelites, 'The LORD [the sacred name, YHWH], the God [Elohim] of your fathers—the God [Elohim] of Abraham, the God [Elohim] of Isaac and the God [Elohim] of Jacob—has sent me to you.' This is my name forever, the name by which I am to be remembered from generation to generation.*"
>
> (Exodus 3:13–15 NIV)

The name *YHWH* has a certain meaning that is related to the name "*I AM*."

The original statement was "*I AM WHO I AM.*" In early Hebrew, when this name was mentioned in the third person, it was,

"He is who He is." However, we have to take another factor into account. In the Hebrew language, the present tense often has a future meaning. So, this name could mean either "I am who I am" or "I will be who I will be." It could mean either "He is who He is" or "He will be who He will be." In other words, the name communicates much more than we can say in one or two simple words.

Aspects of the Name

A Personal God

Let's look at it in this way: *YHWH* essentially means "He is who He is." Grammatically, however, it is more like a personal name—a proper noun rather than a common noun. In this way, it emphasizes God as a Person. This personal name—*Yahweh* or *Jehovah* or *the* LORD, whichever way we want to say it—first occurs in Genesis 2 in connection with the creation of man.

> *The* LORD *God [Jehovah Elohim, or Yahweh Elohim—the two names combined] formed the man from the dust of the ground and breathed into his nostrils the breath of life, and the man became a living being.* (Genesis 2:7 NIV)

The word "*man*" in Hebrew is *adam*. It also is a proper name. So, we see that the proper name *Jehovah*, or *Yahweh* (God) created the proper name *Adam* (a man). This fact brings out the personality of both God and man. A personal God created a personal man. Why? For fellowship between the two.

The use of the name *Jehovah*, or *Yahweh*, in this verse brings out the fact that God, as a Person, created a man, as a person. It brings out right from the beginning God's desire for a Person-to-person relationship with man. We may sum it up in this way: the name *Elohim* indicates God as the general Creator of the universe, while *Jehovah*, or *Yahweh*, indicates Him as the personal Creator of man.

> *A personal God created a personal man for fellowship between the two.*

The first aspect, therefore, of this sacred name is that it is a personal name. It focuses on the fact that God is a real Person. He is not an abstraction, not an entity, not just a supreme being, but a Person.

An Eternal and Unchanging God

The second aspect emphasized by the name *Jehovah*, or *Yahweh*, is that God is eternal and unchanging. This truth is implied by the use of the verb "to be" in Exodus 3:14: "*I AM WHO I AM.*" God is "the one who is." In a certain sense, the "past," "present," and "future" of God all come together in eternity.

This unchanging, eternal nature of Jehovah, or Yahweh, is not only implied, but it is also brought out directly in connection with His name. For example, at the very end of the Old Testament, the Lord Himself brings this out in Malachi's message to Israel, saying,

> For I, the LORD [*Jehovah*, or *Yahweh*], *do not change; therefore you, O sons of Jacob, are not consumed.*　　(Malachi 3:6)

The survival of Israel depends on the eternal, unchanging faithfulness of the Lord.

There is an alternative way to translate that verse, which I actually prefer: "*I am the LORD, I do not change*" (NKJV). That is the very essence of His name. He is the eternal, unchanging One.

This truth is brought out in various ways in the New Testament. The book of Hebrews says of God the Son,

> *Jesus Christ is the same yesterday and today and forever.*
> (Hebrews 13:8 NIV)

Past, present, and future are all rolled together in God. We read in the book of Revelation,

> "*I am the Alpha and the Omega,*" says the Lord God, "*who is, and who was, and who is to come, the Almighty.*"
> (Revelation 1:8 NIV)

There is a transcending of time here. He is the first and the last, the beginning and the end, simultaneously. He is the One "*who is, and who was, and who is to come.*" That phrase is probably the best way of representing the true meaning of the word *Jehovah,* or *Yahweh.* God is not just the one who is in the present, but He also contains within Himself the past and the future.

To sum up, this special, sacred, unique name—*Jehovah,* or *Yahweh*—has two particular significances. First, it emphasizes that God is a Person. Second, it emphasizes that God is the eternal, unchanging One.

3

The One Who Provides

In the previous chapters, we have examined the two great Hebrew names for God found in the Old Testament: (1) *Elohim*, and (2) *Jehovah*, or *Yahweh*. *Elohim* signifies God as the powerful Creator of the universe. *Jehovah*, or *Yahweh*, is the personal name for God.

A God of Covenants

While the two main aspects of the name *Jehovah*, or *Yahweh*, are that God is personal and eternal, this name is also strongly associated with the covenants God makes with men. There are two reasons for this association, and they are related to the aspects of the name noted above.

First, a covenant is a person-to-person relationship. For that reason, it is appropriate that the personal name of God should be used in this connection.

Second, a covenant is unchanging, or permanent. It is therefore appropriate again that the name that emphasizes God's eternal, unchanging nature should be connected with covenants.

Let's look at just two of God's statements about covenants, both of which are found in Psalm 89:

My lovingkindness I will keep for him [David] forever, and My covenant shall be confirmed to him. (verse 28)

My covenant I will not violate, nor will I alter the utterance of My lips. (verse 34)

> ### *Once God has committed Himself to a covenant, He never breaks it.*

Once God has committed Himself to a covenant, He never breaks it. So, again, a covenant is particularly appropriate to associate with the name *Jehovah*, or *Yahweh*, which speaks of the eternal, unchanging nature of God.

The Hebrew word for *"lovingkindness,"* which occurs in verse 28 of the above psalm, is *chesed*, and it is always related to covenant. Personally, the translation I would choose is "God's covenant-keeping faithfulness." It is also translated *"steadfast love"* (RSV) and *"mercy"* (KJV). But I believe we understand it properly only when we relate God's lovingkindness to His covenant; it is that aspect of God's nature that holds Him to His covenant.

Seven Covenantal Names of God

The name *Jehovah*, or *Yahweh*, is directly linked with seven specific names, or titles, representing seven aspects of God's covenant-keeping faithfulness in His dealings with man. In the order of their occurrence in the Scriptures, these names reveal Jehovah in the following aspects:

1. The One Who Provides

2. The One Who Heals

3. The One Who Is Our Banner

4. The One Who Is Our Peace

5. The One Who Is Our Shepherd

6. The One Who Is Our Righteousness

7. The One Who Is There (Permanently Present)

The First Covenantal Name of God: The One Who Provides

We will explore each of these covenantal names of the Lord in succession, beginning with *The One Who Provides*. This name is mentioned first in Genesis 22 in the story of Abraham taking his son Isaac to Mount Moriah, where he was willing to offer him as a sacrifice to the Lord. When they arrived at the foot of the mountain, Abraham told his servants to remain there with the donkey while he took Isaac and the fire for the burnt offering. Abraham and his son went up the mountain together. This is what followed:

> *And Abraham took the wood of the burnt offering and laid it on Isaac his son, and he took in his hand the fire and the knife. So the two of them walked on together. And Isaac spoke to Abraham his father and said, "My father!" And he said, "Here I am, my son." And he said, "Behold, the fire and the wood, but where is the lamb for the burnt offering?" And Abraham said, "God will provide for Himself the lamb for the burnt offering, my son." So the two of them walked on together.*
> (Genesis 22:6–8)

After they had come to the top of the mountain and Abraham had prepared his son as the sacrifice, at the last moment, God intervened and told him that He did not require the sacrifice of Isaac. Instead, Abraham sacrificed a ram that he found caught by its horns in a thicket. (See verses 9–13.) Then, we read the part where the name appears:

> *And Abraham called the name of that place The LORD Will Provide, as it is said to this day, "In the mount of the LORD it will be provided."*
> (verse 14)

That is where the first covenant name of Jehovah, or Yahweh, appears—Jehovah the provider, the One who will provide. (English-speaking people tend to say *Jehovah Jireh*. However, that pronunciation is very remote from how it sounds in Hebrew.)

In Hebrew, the word that is translated "*Provide*" is literally "to see." From that meaning, we get this beautiful thought that when God sees, He provides. We also get the wonderful concept that God's first covenant commitment is to provide. This is the root of all His commitment: He provides for His people.

The Outworking of God's Provision

Let's look at the outworking of this covenant commitment of the Lord to provide for His people. It is a most beautiful picture as we see it worked out in the subsequent revelation of Scripture. It points us to one Person who is the fulfillment of all God's covenant commitments: Jesus the Messiah.

Note some particular points. First, the primary provision was a lamb. Isaac said, "*Where is the lamb?*" (Genesis 22:7), and Abraham replied, "*God will provide for Himself the lamb*" (verse 8). When the fulfillment of the commitment came, it was a lamb—the Lamb of God. This is how John the Baptist spoke of Jesus:

> *The next day he* [John the Baptist] *saw Jesus coming to him, and said, "Behold, the Lamb of God who takes away the sin of the world!"* (John 1:29)

God fulfilled Abraham's confidence in Him. Two thousand years later, He provided the Lamb, the ultimate sacrifice—the One in whom all of God's covenant commitments were fulfilled. When you think about the name "*The LORD Will Provide*" (Genesis 22:14), always let it carry your mind to that Lamb through whom the provision was made. "The Lord will provide a lamb for the sacrifice." When Jesus came, He was the provided lamb, "*the Lamb of God who takes away the sin of the world.*"

Scripture says in that incident with Abraham, *"In the mount of the LORD it will be provided"* (Genesis 22:14). Again, this is fascinating as we trace its outworking. Moriah is generally agreed to be the same mountain that occurs in the New Testament as Golgotha or Calvary. So, on the very mountain where Abraham made that original confession of his faith, *"God will provide for Himself the lamb"* (verse 8), and where it was said later, *"In the mount of the LORD it will be provided"* (verse 14), two thousand years later, it was provided by the death of Jesus on the cross.

Jesus was the provided lamb, "the Lamb of God who takes away the sin of the world."

That was the ultimate provision of God for the need—not only of Abraham and of the Jewish people, but also of the whole seed of Abraham, of all those who believe in God.

Types and Pictures of God's Provision

Abraham and Isaac and the sacrifice on Mount Moriah are beautiful types of what took place at Calvary. Abraham typifies God the Father, Isaac typifies God the Son, the fire for the sacrifice typifies the Holy Spirit, and the wood Isaac carried typifies the cross.

There is the whole scene of the crucifixion in preview: Abraham, the father, offering his only son, Isaac; the fire of the Spirit needed to make the sacrifice possible; and the wood on which the sacrifice was to take place.

We can sum all of this up in one verse of the New Testament:

He who did not spare His own Son, but delivered Him up for us all, how will He not also with Him freely give us all things?
(Romans 8:32)

There is the total commitment: "*The LORD will provide*" (Genesis 22:14)—not just in one situation or for one need, but in every situation, for every need, for time and for eternity.

The Lord has made a covenant commitment associated with His own divine, personal, unchanging name. He will always provide for His people. The ultimate proof and the ultimate provision is in the Son of God, the Lord Jesus Christ, who became the sin offering, "*the Lamb of God who takes away the sin of the world*" (John 1:29).

Would you take a moment now and meditate on this verse?

He who did not spare His own Son, but delivered Him up for us all, how will He not also with Him freely give us all things?

Remember, it is "*with Him.*" You cannot have the provision without the Lamb. The provision is in the Lamb of God—Jesus.

4

The One Who Heals

We have seen that God's name *Jehovah*, or *Yahweh*, is directly linked with seven specific names, or titles, representing seven aspects of God's covenant-keeping faithfulness in His dealings with man. In the previous chapter, we looked at the first of these covenantal names, *The One Who Provides*. I pointed out that God's first commitment to His people is to provide. Now, we are going to deal with the second covenantal name, *The One Who Heals*.

"I, The Lord, Am Your Healer"

This name is first found in Exodus 15, which relates an experience of the Israelites in their deliverance from Egypt. They had just crossed the Red Sea and set out on their journey through the wilderness:

Then Moses led Israel from the Red Sea, and they went out into the wilderness of Shur; and they went three days in the wilderness and found no water. And when they came to Marah, they could not drink the waters of Marah, for they were bitter; therefore it was named Marah [bitter]. So the people grumbled at Moses, saying, "What shall we drink?" Then he cried out to the LORD, and the LORD showed him a tree; and

he threw it into the waters, and the waters became sweet. There He made for them a statute and regulation, and there He tested them. And He said, "If you will give earnest heed to the voice of the LORD your God, and do what is right in His sight, and give ear to His commandments, and keep all His statutes, I will put none of the diseases on you which I have put on the Egyptians; for I, the LORD [Jehovah], am your healer."
(Exodus 15:22–26)

> *"I, the Lord, am your healer." It would be perfectly correct to translate this as "I am Jehovah, your doctor."*

The second covenantal name of God is given at the very end of the passage: *"the LORD...your healer."*

The word that is translated *"healer"* is the basic Hebrew word for "physical healing." In modern Hebrew, it is the word used for "doctor." In fact, it would be perfectly correct to translate this as "I am Jehovah, your doctor." That is exactly what it would be in contemporary Hebrew. *"The LORD"* (*Jehovah*, or *Yahweh*) is directly connected to the word for one who heals. Alternatively, we could say, "The Lord who heals."

Let's focus on some significant points of the above account.

Significant Lessons from the Healing at Marah

It Is Wiser to Pray than Grumble

First, it always strikes me that in the crisis described in Exodus 15:22–26, about three million people grumbled while one man prayed. And Moses got the solution. This reminds us that it is always wiser to pray than to grumble. The Scripture says,

> *Do all things without grumbling or disputing; that you may prove yourselves to be blameless and innocent, children of God*

*above reproach in the midst of a crooked and perverse genera-
tion, among whom you appear as lights in the world, holding
fast the word of life.* (Philippians 2:14–16)

God Decided to Be His People's Healer

Second, the initiative in this revelation came from God. There
is so much skepticism today in the church about God's power and
willingness to heal. We need to see that God set up a teaching situation: He brought His people to the point of desperation, and then,
out of His own will and counsel, He specifically revealed Himself
as the healer of His people. It was not something that the people
asked for. It was something that came from God's own decision.
God Himself decided to be the healer of His people.

It Takes Faith to Release God's Power

Third, it is important to recognize that it took an act of faith
to release God's miracle-working power—as it usually does. God
showed Moses a certain tree. Moses had to pick up the tree and cast
it into the water. That act of faith—casting the tree into the water—
released God's miracle-working power in that water.

Moses could have stood on the brink of the water and just "believed" without doing anything, and nothing would ever have happened. This brings out the principle that "*faith without works is
dead*" (James 2:26). If we believe, we need to demonstrate our faith
through our words, actions, or both.

The Tree Points to the Cross

Fourth, we also need to see that the tree was the means of healing those bitter waters. In Hebrew, the word *tree* is used both for a
tree that is growing and for a tree that has already been cut down.
In the New Testament, in a number of translations, the word *tree*
is used for the cross. (See, for example, Acts 5:30 NIV, KJV, NKJV,
RSV.) Once again, the Marah account points us forward to the
cross of Jesus as the place where this healing covenant found its
ultimate fulfillment.

Ask "What?" Rather Than "Why?"

Another aspect that always impresses me is that we are never told why the waters were bitter. But Moses was shown how to make them sweet. Sometimes, we waste our energy in life by asking a lot of unfruitful questions, such as "Why did this or that happen?" We must bypass those questions, go to God, and say, "Lord, show me what to do." And God will do it. Understanding why things have happened would just burden our minds. But God will always give us the practical answer when we want to know what to do.

Requirements for Healing

Wholehearted Faith in God

The basic requirement for healing is stated clearly: *"If you will give earnest heed to the voice of the LORD your God…"* (Exodus 15:26). In the original Hebrew, it is literally, "If listening you will listen to the voice of the LORD." The word *listen* is repeated twice.

Once, as I lay sick in a hospital, desperately needing healing and seeking God for it in the Scriptures, this verse came to me. I said, "What does it mean to 'listen, listening'?" And it seemed God gave me this answer: "I gave you two ears, a right ear and a left ear. To 'listen, listening' is to listen to Me with both ears. But if you listen to Me with one ear and to somebody else with the other ear, all you get is confusion and not faith." So, I stopped up my ear to the sinister whisper of the devil and listened to God with both ears. Sure enough, I received my healing!

Trust in Jesus' Fulfillment of God's Covenant

In the last chapter, we saw that God's commitment to provide found its fulfillment in Jesus, the Lamb of God. The same is true of God's commitment to heal. It, too, found its final fulfillment in Jesus. This is the record of the New Testament:

And when evening had come, they brought to Him [Jesus] many who were demon-possessed; and He cast out the spirits with a

word, and healed all who were ill in order that what was spoken through Isaiah the prophet might be fulfilled, saying, "He Himself took our infirmities, and carried away our diseases."
(Matthew 8:16–17)

Jesus was the final fulfillment of the healing covenant of God for His people. On the cross, Jesus not only bore our sin, but He also took our infirmities and carried away our diseases. He not only provided forgiveness, but He also provided healing.

His provision was not only in the spiritual realm, but also in the physical realm. That was a covenant commitment God had made with Israel. For this reason, we do not read in the New Testament that any Israelite ever came to Jesus for healing and was refused. There is no record of any Israelite ever being refused healing. For instance, read this account:

— ⤳ —

Jesus not only provided forgiveness, but He also provided healing.

— ⤳ —

And when the men of that place recognized Him, they sent into all that surrounding district and brought to Him all who were sick; and they began to entreat Him that they might just touch the fringe of His cloak; and as many as touched it were cured.
(Matthew 14:35–36)

The people just had to touch His cloak and they were healed. However, Jesus' attitude toward Gentiles, those who were not Jewish, was different. In Matthew 15, we read about a Canaanite woman who was not Jewish but who began to cry out for Him to have mercy on her daughter. She said,

"Lord, Son of David; my daughter is cruelly demon-possessed." But He [Jesus] did not answer her a word. And His disciples came to Him and kept asking Him, saying, "Send her away, for she is shouting out after us." But He answered and

said, "I was sent only to the lost sheep of the house of Israel."
(Matthew 15:22–24)

In other words, "My covenant obligation is not to those who are not of the house of Israel."

But she came and began to bow down before Him, saying, "Lord, help me!" And He answered and said, "It is not good to take the children's bread and throw it to the dogs."
(verses 5–26)

Unless we understand the nature of covenant commitment, it is hard to understand Jesus' reply. Jesus had a covenant with Israel by which He was committed to be their healer. Therefore, healing was the children's bread. This woman had no covenant, no claim. Oh, but she had faith!

She said, "Yes, Lord; but even the dogs feed on the crumbs which fall from their masters' table." (verse 27)

Think of the significance of her statement. She said, in effect, "Lord, I don't need a slice. All I need is a crumb. One little crumb will do all that's needed for my daughter." Jesus' response is one of the most beautiful in Scripture.

Then Jesus answered and said to her, "O woman, your faith is great; be it done for you as you wish." And her daughter was healed at once. (verse 28)

The woman's faith called forth Jesus' compassion, even though He had no covenantal obligation.

Remember that God is *still* the healer of His people. The blessings of the covenant are now available to both Jews and Gentiles—to all those who come in faith, through Jesus, to God the Father, on the basis of His covenantal name: *The One Who Heals.*

For I, the LORD, am your healer. (Exodus 15:26)

Christ redeemed us from the curse of the Law, having become a curse for us—for it is written, "Cursed is everyone who hangs on a tree"—in order that in Christ Jesus the blessing of Abraham might come to the Gentiles, so that we might receive the promise of the Spirit through faith.

(Galatians 3:13–14)

5

The One Who Is Our Banner

This covenantal name of Jehovah, or Yahweh, *The One Who Is Our Banner*, is found in the book of Exodus. It is mentioned in connection with an incident experienced by the Israelites on their way through the desert to the Promised Land after coming out of Egypt. One of the Gentile nations, the Amalekites, came and sought to oppose the Israelites' journey to their inheritance. They had to fight to continue their journey. Eventually, they succeeded in defeating the Amalekites, and they were able to continue their journey. Here is the record of this incident:

> *Then Amalek came and fought against Israel at Rephidim....So Joshua overwhelmed Amalek and his people with the edge of the sword. Then the LORD said to Moses, "Write this in a book as a memorial, and recite it to Joshua, that I will utterly blot out the memory of Amalek from under heaven." And Moses built an altar, and named it The LORD [Jehovah] is My Banner; and he said, "The LORD has sworn; the LORD will have war against Amalek from generation to generation."* (Exodus 17:8, 13–16)

Opposition Is Inevitable

This particular episode is invested with a permanent significance because the lesson, as I see it, is this: in our journey to, and in our attempt to enter into, the inheritance God has provided for us, we are always going to face opposition. This is not just something that

The Lord is going to stand with us in the opposition, but we are going to have to participate in these battles.

happened once; it is going to happen from generation to generation. The Lord is going to take our side. He is going to stand with us in the opposition, but we are going to have to participate in these battles.

The particular aspect of the Lord's help that is brought out in the above passage is found in the name of the altar that Moses built: "*The Lord is My Banner*" (Exodus 17:15). We see that the Lord has given us a banner that will bring us victory in the warfare we have to go through.

There is much written in the New Testament about this warfare. For instance, Paul wrote,

> For our struggle is not against flesh and blood, but against the rulers, against the powers, against the world forces of this darkness, against the spiritual forces of wickedness in the heavenly places.　　　　　　　　　　(Ephesians 6:12)

In other words, we, as Christians, are going to encounter opposition and warfare. Our war will not be with physical enemies but with spiritual, satanic forces that will oppose our spiritual journeys.

In 2 Corinthians, Paul talked about the type of weapons we need in this warfare:

> For though we walk in the flesh, we do not war according to the flesh, for the weapons of our warfare are not of the flesh, but divinely powerful for the destruction of fortresses.
> 　　　　　　　　　　　　　　(2 Corinthians 10:3–4)

"*Not of the flesh*" means that our weapons are, in effect, the opposite of the flesh—they are spiritual. So, God has provided us with spiritual weapons for a spiritual warfare.

Our Banner Is the Name of the Lord

In Psalm 20:5, in particular, we hear about the banner the Lord has provided:

We will sing for joy over your victory, and in the name of our God we will set up our banners.

Our banner is the name of the Lord our God, and His victory becomes our victory as we set up our banners in His name.

There is much to learn, of course, about the name of the Lord in the New Testament. For instance, Paul said this about Jesus:

Therefore also God highly exalted Him, and bestowed on Him the name which is above every name, that at the name of Jesus every knee should bow, of those who are in heaven, and on earth, and under the earth, and that every tongue should confess that Jesus Christ is Lord, to the glory of God the Father.
(Philippians 2:9–11)

In the name of the Lord Jesus Christ, then, we have a banner before which all the forces of evil have to bow and yield. In this way, Paul said, Christ's victory becomes our victory.

But thanks be to God, who always leads us in His triumph in Christ, and manifests through us the sweet aroma of the knowledge of Him in every place. (2 Corinthians 2:14)

The victory that Christ won over Satan on the cross is made available to us on the condition that we use the banner that God has provided. The banner is the name of the Lord Jesus Christ. So, the name of the Lord is our banner in this spiritual war.

Our Standard-Bearer

As we continue to look at our banner, the name of the Lord, I want to use Old Testament Scriptures and history to highlight the significance of the standard-bearer—the one who carried the banner, or standard, in an ancient army. Describing the defeat of a large Gentile force, the Assyrian army, the prophet Isaiah said,

They shall be as when a standardbearer fainteth.

(Isaiah 10:18 KJV)

When a standard-bearer fainted, the whole army would become disorganized. Ancient armies were trained to regroup around the standard. If they were hard-pressed in battle, they were liable to be divided and separated from one another. The standard-bearer would find some kind of eminence, a hill or other high ground, and lift up the standard. But if the standard-bearer fainted, there was no place for the soldiers to regroup. That meant a very serious problem for the army.

In our case, as Christians, our Standard-Bearer is the Holy Spirit. Isaiah said,

So shall they fear the name of the LORD from the west, and his glory from the rising of the sun. When the enemy shall come in like a flood, the Spirit of the LORD shall lift up a standard against him. (Isaiah 59:19 KJV)

The Spirit of the Lord, the Holy Spirit, is our Standard-Bearer when we are hard-pressed in this Christian warfare by the forces of Satan, and they are coming like a flood against us. Our Standard-Bearer lifts up the standard—the name of the Lord Jesus Christ.

Then, we regroup around that standard. When we see the name of the Lord Jesus uplifted, we gather there. The name of Jesus is our rallying point.

The name of Jesus is our rallying point.

Today, all across the earth, the Holy Spirit is lifting up afresh the standard of the name of the Lord Jesus Christ. God's people are rallying to that standard, irrespective of church denomination and other factors that have separated them.

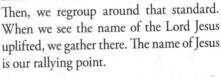

The Victorious Church

Finally, look at this picture in the Song of Solomon of the victorious church, which came into being in the New Testament through the atoning work of Christ:

You are as beautiful as Tirzah, my darling, as lovely as Jerusalem, as awesome as an army with banners...."Who is this that grows like the dawn, as beautiful as the full moon, as pure as the sun, as awesome as an army with banners?"
(Song of Solomon 6:4, 10)

Described here is the church as the bride of Christ. But it is the army of Christ, as well.

It is also very interesting to note the two closing pictures of Christians in the epistle of the Ephesians: the bride (see Ephesians 5:25–32) and the army (see Ephesians 6:10–17). We are both the bride and the army, and we are going to come forth on the stage of history as prophesied in the Song of Solomon—like an army, awesome with its banner: the name of the Lord Jesus Christ.

6

The One Who Is Our Peace

We will now address a fourth covenantal name of Jehovah, or Yahweh: *The One Who Is Our Peace.* This name is revealed in Judges 6 through an incident in the life of Gideon.

"Peace to You"

In Gideon's time, the Midianites, who belonged to a Gentile nation from the east, had overrun the land of the Israelites and were grievously oppressing them. The Israelites were living almost like refugees in their own land. Gideon, a young man, was surreptitiously threshing wheat in a winepress in order to hide it from the Midianites, because they would have taken the wheat from him if they had seen him.

Suddenly, *"the angel of the LORD"* (Judges 6:11) appeared to Gideon and told him that he was to become the Lord's instrument to defeat the Midianites and to deliver the Israelites. Gideon found this very hard to believe—he thought he was inadequate for the task. But the angel of the Lord told him that he would be a *"mighty man of valor"* (verse 12 NKJV) and gave him the strategy by which he was to conquer the Midianites.

Toward the end of this encounter, Gideon wanted to know more about the angel who had appeared to him, and he wanted to offer a sacrifice. This is where we'll pick up the story:

> *So Gideon said to Him* [the Lord], *"If now I have found favor*
> *in Thy sight, then show me a sign that it is Thou who speakest*
> *with me. Please do not depart from here, until I come back to*
> *Thee, and bring out my offering and lay it before Thee." And*
> *He said, "I will remain until you return." Then Gideon went*
> *in and prepared a kid and unleavened bread from an ephah of*
> *flour; he put the meat in a basket and the broth in a pot, and*
> *brought them out to him under the oak, and presented them.*
> *And the angel of God said to him, "Take the meat and the un-*
> *leavened bread and lay them on this rock, and pour out the*
> *broth." And he* [Gideon] *did so. Then the angel of the* LORD *put*
> *out the end of the staff that was in his hand and touched the*
> *meat and the unleavened bread; and fire sprang up from the*
> *rock and consumed the meat and the unleavened bread. Then*
> *the angel of the* LORD *vanished from his sight. When Gideon saw*
> *that he was the angel of the* LORD, *he said, "Alas, O Lord* GOD!
> *For now I have seen the angel of the* LORD *face to face." And the*
> LORD *said to him, "Peace to you, do not fear; you shall not die."*
> (Judges 6:17–23)

It was generally believed at that time that if you were to see an angel of the Lord, you would probably not survive the sight. So, Gideon
felt that his last moment had come. But the Lord said to him, "Don't
fear. You're not going to die." In gratitude for this, and as a response
to the revelation he had received, Gideon built an altar.

> *Then Gideon built an altar there to the* LORD *and named it*
> *The* LORD [*Jehovah*] *is Peace. To this day it is still in Ophrah*
> *of the Abiezrites.* (Judges 6:24)

Most of us are familiar with the Hebrew word for peace—it is
shalom. It is the contemporary greeting in Hebrew. That was the
name of the altar: The LORD is *shalom*, peace. Here, therefore, is revealed to us the fourth aspect of the Lord's covenant-keeping faithfulness to His people—that He is His people's peace. Peace is in a
person, and that Person is the Lord Himself.

Three Ways in Which God Provides Peace

There are three ways in which we need peace. First, we need peace with God, a personal relationship with the Lord that assures us His favor and His blessing. In Scripture, peace with God is always assured only through a sacrifice. Apart from a sacrifice—a life laid down and a shedding of blood—there can be no peace with God. (See Hebrews 9:22.)

In Scripture, peace with God is always assured only through a sacrifice.

Second, we need peace not just in our relationships with God, but also in the midst of all that we find coming against us. Even in the midst of war and tumult, God offers His people peace. Peace is not just the absence of war. Actually, it is possible to have peace in the midst of war, conflict, pressure, and turmoil because peace is based on a relationship with God, not on circumstances. If you look at your circumstances, many times you find that there is no cause for peace. But if you have learned the truth contained in this covenant name of Jehovah—that He is our peace—then you can have that peace in the midst of any circumstances in which you find yourself.

Third, we need peace in our relationships with other people. Being reconciled to God through Jesus brings us into relationships of peace with other believers.

Let's look at peace, then, from these three points of view: first, in our relationship with the Lord; second, in the outworking of that relationship in our lives in the midst of our circumstances; and third, in our relationships with others.

Peace with God

We will begin with what Scripture has to say about peace between God and man. There is much about that topic in the New Testament, but we will look at only two passages.

Therefore having been justified by faith, we have peace with God through our Lord Jesus Christ. (Romans 5:1)

Notice that it says "*peace with God through our Lord Jesus Christ.*" Jesus is our peace.

For it was the Father's good pleasure for all the fulness to dwell in Him [Jesus], and through Him to reconcile all things to Himself, having made peace through the blood of His cross; through Him, I say, whether things on earth or things in heaven. (Colossians 1:19–20)

In this passage, we see the second aspect of that truth: peace is achieved only by sacrifice. The sacrifice that finally achieved eternal peace between God and man was the sacrifice of the Lord Jesus on the cross and the blood that He shed. Through Him, we have peace with God.

Contrast peace through Christ with what Isaiah said:

But the wicked are like the tossing sea, for it cannot be quiet, and its waters toss up refuse and mud. "There is no peace," says my God, "for the wicked." (Isaiah 57:20–21)

There is a very definite dividing line between the righteous and the wicked. Those who are reconciled with God through Jesus Christ receive His righteousness and know what it is to have peace with God. But for the wicked, God says, "*There is no peace.*"

Sin never leaves us in peace. Even though there may be nothing troublesome in our outward circumstances, there is something in our hearts that can never rest while sin rules our hearts.

Peace in Difficult Circumstances

Now we will look at the second outworking of peace, the peace that we can have in the midst of tumult and war. Oh, how important it is to have this kind of peace in today's world!

Jesus said to His disciples,

Peace I leave with you; My peace I give to you; not as the world gives, do I give to you. Let not your heart be troubled, nor let it be fearful. (John 14:27)

I have always been glad for the words "*not as the world gives.*" The world's most strenuous attempts at peace are so fragile, so impermanent, and so unsatisfying. If we depended on the world for our peace, we would indeed have very little. But Jesus said, "I give you a peace that's not the same as the world gives, and you don't need to be fearful or troubled."

He also said in John 16:33,

These things I have spoken to you, that in Me you may have peace. In the world you have tribulation, but take courage; I have overcome the world.

Jesus is our peace. He has overcome the world. Therefore, the world can never overcome us because He is in us and with us.

Peace with Other Believers

Third, being reconciled to God through Jesus brings us into relationships of peace with other believers. We have peace with those who have been reconciled to Jesus, regardless of who they are, no matter what race and background they come from. In writing to believers who had a Gentile background, Paul said,

But now in Christ Jesus you who formerly were far off have been brought near by the blood of Christ. For He Himself is our peace, who made both groups into one, and broke down the barrier of the dividing wall, by abolishing in His flesh the enmity, which is the Law of commandments contained in ordinances, that in Himself He might make the two into one new man, thus establishing peace, and might reconcile them both in one body to God through the cross, by it having put to death the enmity. And He came and preached peace to you who were far away, and peace to those who were near. (Ephesians 2:13–17)

The Ark: A Picture of Peace in Christ

The message of the cross is peace: peace with God, peace in the midst of turmoil, and peace with our fellow believers.

I am always reminded of the ark, which became God's means of salvation to Noah and his family. Think of Noah and his family in this ark. There they were, in the midst of the raging elements; everything around them had gone under the water. Yet, in the ark, they had peace and security.

Then, think about all those animals in the ark. They were animals of such different types, animals that were, by nature, enemies of one another. But in the ark there was peace. That tells me that when those animals entered into the ark, they underwent a change of nature.

When we enter into Christ, we enter into peace.

Thus, the ark, to me, is a beautiful picture of Christ. When we enter into Christ, we enter into peace. In the church, there are those of different races whom, under natural conditions, we might have hated. Yet, because we are in that ark, we know peace with them. And in the midst of the raging turmoil of this life, we know peace in our hearts because we have peace with God through the Lord who is our peace.

7

The One Who Is Our Shepherd

We will now look at the fifth of these covenantal names: *The One Who Is Our Shepherd*. For this name, I turn to one of the most familiar passages in the Scriptures, Psalm 23, often called "The Shepherd's Psalm." Let us work our way through the verses of this psalm in order.

The Shepherd Meets Every Need

The LORD *[Jehovah] is my shepherd, I shall not want.*
(Psalm 23:1)

When I look at this verse, I am amazed at how much Scripture can say in so few words—particularly in the original Hebrew. It might interest you to know that in Hebrew, the entire first verse of Psalm 23 consists of only four words: YHWH *raah—"the Lord is my shepherd,"* and *lo chaser—"I shall not want."* Think how much is contained in those four Hebrew words.

"I shall not want" is the most amazing statement, isn't it? Every need that could ever arise in life will be met. Never will we find ourselves in a situation where something we really need is not available to us. The Lord has guaranteed to give us all that we need. Out of His relationship with us, and ours with Him, *"The Lord is my shepherd, I shall not want."*

The Living Bible (TLB) says it this way: "*Because the Lord is my Shepherd, I have everything I need!*" Think of all that is contained in the beautiful words "*the Lord is my shepherd.*" It is very important that we understand we have a personal relationship with God as a Person. This fact is the basis for everything else.

It is also an individual relationship. David said, "*The Lord is **my** shepherd.*" It is very direct and very personal. In Psalm 80, another psalm of David, he wrote,

> *Oh, give ear, Shepherd of Israel, Thou who dost lead Joseph like a flock; Thou who art enthroned above the cherubim, shine forth!* (Psalm 80:1)

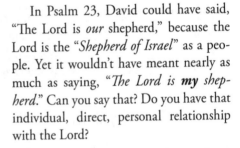
Do you have an individual, direct, personal relationship with the Lord?

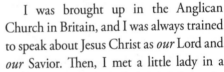

In Psalm 23, David could have said, "The Lord is *our* shepherd," because the Lord is the "*Shepherd of Israel*" as a people. Yet it wouldn't have meant nearly as much as saying, "*The Lord is **my** shepherd.*" Can you say that? Do you have that individual, direct, personal relationship with the Lord?

I was brought up in the Anglican Church in Britain, and I was always trained to speak about Jesus Christ as *our* Lord and *our* Savior. Then, I met a little lady in a humble home, and she said, "*My* Lord." And a little while later, she said, "*My* Savior."

I thought to myself, *I can't say that. I don't have that relationship. In a general way, I can say, "Our Lord" and "Our Savior." But I don't understand how she can say, "My Lord" and "My Savior."* Thank God, I came to understand; I came to have that relationship. It's individual, it's personal, and it's direct. "*The Lord is **my** shepherd.*"

Let's look in the rest of the psalm at what flows out of this personal relationship with the Lord.

The Shepherd Gives...

Nourishment and Refreshment

He makes me lie down in green pastures; He leads me beside quiet waters. (Psalm 23:2)

The Lord provides all the nourishment that I need. Of course, we are thinking primarily in terms of spiritual nourishment. He gives me clear, pure water and fresh, clean grass. Everything is clean, fresh, and health-giving.

Restoration

He restores my soul. (Psalm 23:3)

I love the word *restore*. It means to put back in the right condition, to refresh, to renew. Do you ever feel jaded and tired, worn and frayed? Do you know that it is possible to have your soul restored? Do you know that the Lord can put you back to freshness, confidence, and strength?

Guidance

He guides me in the paths of righteousness for His name's sake. (Psalm 23:3)

The Lord guides us in the paths of righteousness. He makes sure that we follow the right way. There are so many ways in life, so many choices. Do you ever feel confused and uncertain as to which road to take? When you know the Lord as your Shepherd, He leads you and guides you in the paths of righteousness.

Then, it says, *"For His name's sake."* That blesses me, too, because His name does not change. It does not depend on whether I am weak or strong; it depends on His name. His honor is at stake. He has guaranteed that He is going to do it. His name is attached to the very word *shepherd*—the Lord my Shepherd.

The Shepherd Is with Us in Life's Valleys

Even though I walk through the valley of the shadow of death, I fear no evil; for Thou art with me; Thy rod and Thy staff, they comfort me. (Psalm 23:4)

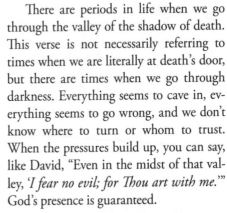

When the pressures build up, you can say, "I fear no evil; for Thou art with me."

There are periods in life when we go through the valley of the shadow of death. This verse is not necessarily referring to times when we are literally at death's door, but there are times when we go through darkness. Everything seems to cave in, everything seems to go wrong, and we don't know where to turn or whom to trust. When the pressures build up, you can say, like David, "Even in the midst of that valley, '*I fear no evil; for Thou art with me.*'" God's presence is guaranteed.

David continued, "*Thy rod and Thy staff, they comfort me.*" Two aspects of God's presence are represented here. The "*rod*" represents the Lord's protection over us from outside attacks and His loving discipline of us when we go astray. The "*staff*" represents the Lord's guidance and direction. Both the rod and the staff bring us comfort because we know, and have experienced, that God will protect, correct, and lead us, even in the midst of the dark, lonely valleys.

For one entire year, I lay in a hospital with a disease that doctors were not able to cure. Believe me, it was a long, dark, lonely valley. But the Lord was with me through it all, and He brought me out at the other end stronger than I had ever been before. The Lord is my Shepherd.

The Shepherd Supplies Overflowing Provision

Thou dost prepare a table before me in the presence of my enemies; Thou hast anointed my head with oil; my cup overflows. (Psalm 23:5)

What a blessing it is to know that all this takes place in the presence of our enemies. Right there, where everything is against us, God provides the best. He spreads a banquet; He prepares a table.

Picture our enemies like wolves out in the darkness, scared away by the light of the campfire, prowling around but afraid to come into the light. It is here that God provides His best.

It is good to have a banquet provided by the Lord, no matter where He provides it. But it is especially good to have it in the presence of your enemies. Because the Lord is there, and because He is the Shepherd, we know that they cannot touch us; we are safe even in the presence of our enemies.

Then, David said, *"Thou hast anointed my head with oil; my cup overflows."* We do not merely have enough for ourselves, but we also have enough to share with others.

The Shepherd Grants Goodness and Lovingkindness

Surely goodness and lovingkindness will follow me all the days of my life. (Psalm 23:6)

No matter what situations we find ourselves in or what we have to go through, there are two unchangeable factors in our lives: the goodness of the Lord and the lovingkindness of the Lord. Again, the word *"lovingkindness"* in Hebrew is *chesed*. It particularly means "the faithfulness of God to His covenant commitment." So, the Lord has committed to be my Shepherd. He will never break His covenant. His goodness and lovingkindness are always with me.

The Shepherd Brings Us All the Way Home

And I will dwell in the house of the LORD forever. (Psalm 23:6)

Consider the meaning of this last sentence, *"I will dwell in the house of the Lord forever."* That verse suggests to me that whatever I'm doing, and wherever I'm going, I'm on my way home. I am going home to the place the Lord has provided for me.

I used to live in the middle of a city on a little island that had just one road in and out. As you approached the bridge going onto that little island, there was a sign that read DEAD END because there was no exit. I used to look at that sign and say to myself, *It may well be a dead end for some people, but for me, it is the way home.*

That is how it is when you know the Lord. What others call a dead end is, for you, the way home. You know that you are going to be living in the house of the Lord forever, no matter what you have to go through. He will be with you, and you will know your destination.

Dead ends are for the people who don't know God. There are no dead ends for you. You are on your way home.

8

The One Who Is Our Righteousness

The sixth of the covenantal names of God is *The One Who Is Our Righteousness.* This name is found in one of the many promises of restoration given to Israel through the prophets—all of which center on the Messiah. Let us look at one of these promises in Jeremiah:

> *"Behold, the days are coming,"* declares the LORD, *"when I shall raise up for David a righteous Branch* [one of the common titles of Messiah in the Old Testament]; *and He will reign as king and act wisely and do justice and righteousness in the land. In his days Judah will be saved, and Israel will dwell securely; and this is His name by which He will be called, 'The LORD* [Jehovah] *our righteousness.'"*
> (Jeremiah 23:5–6)

Restoration includes the reestablishment of righteousness. In fact, without righteousness, other forms of restoration would be ultimately impossible or worthless.

God is going to restore righteousness to His people. But the righteousness that He has promised to restore is in a Person. Our righteousness is not in a system of law or in a religion; rather, it is in a person—and that Person is the promised Messiah.

63

Two Kinds of Righteousness

Self-Righteousness

It is important to see that there are two kinds of righteousness. One is our own righteousness—what we would call self-righteousness—which is not acceptable to God. Isaiah said,

> *For all of us have become like one who is unclean, and all our righteous deeds are like a filthy garment.*   (Isaiah 64:6)

We could easily understand if Isaiah had said, "All our *sins* are like a filthy garment." But he said, *"All our righteous deeds are like a filthy garment."* In other words, even the best that we can achieve in our own righteousness is totally unacceptable to God. It falls far below the standard of righteousness God requires.

We are faced with two alternatives: having either the kind of righteousness we achieve by our own efforts or the kind of righteousness we receive in a Person, in the Messiah Jesus. They are mutually exclusive; we cannot offer both to God.

Righteousness through Faith in Christ

This was Paul's determination, as recorded in Philippians 3:8–9:

> *That I...may be found in Him* [Jesus Christ, the Messiah], *not having a righteousness of my own derived from the Law, but that which is through faith in Christ, the righteousness which comes from God on the basis of faith.*

Notice that Paul had to renounce the kind of righteousness he could achieve by his own effort in order to obtain the righteousness that comes through faith in Jesus Christ. You see, the great mistake the Israelites made in their history—the one that had such a harmful effect on their destiny for two thousand years—is that they sought the wrong kind of righteousness. Paul explained this in Romans:

> *For not knowing about God's righteousness, and seeking to establish their own* [righteousness], *they did not subject*

themselves to the righteousness of God. For Christ is the end of the law for righteousness to everyone who believes.
(Romans 10:3–4)

It is important to see that the death of Christ on the cross expiated the sins and shortcomings of all who had failed to observe the law. It also provided another means of righteousness, which is through faith in Christ. Those who seek to establish their own righteousness do not subject themselves to the righteousness of God through Christ and, therefore, are not made righteous.

The Process and the Exchange

The phrase *"did not subject themselves"* (Romans 10:3) indicates that there is a kind of self-humbling that we must go through in order to obtain *"the righteousness of God"* (verse 3). First, we must renounce our own righteousness, acknowledging that our own efforts have not achieved what God requires. Then, we must accept God's offer of mercy and righteousness through faith in the atoning death of Jesus Christ.

> *We must acknowledge that our own efforts have not achieved what God requires.*

Paul spoke about the righteousness that is made available to us through Christ:

He [God] *made Him* [Jesus] *who knew no sin to be sin on our behalf, that we might become the righteousness of God in Him.* (2 Corinthians 5:21)

An exchange was made at the cross: Jesus was made sin with our sinfulness. He became the sin offering, the great *"guilt offering"* that was promised in Isaiah 53:10. His soul became the sin offering. He became sin for us so that we might receive the other aspect of the exchange: becoming the righteousness of God in Him. How foolish it is to cling to our own righteousness when we can have, by faith, the righteousness of God in Christ.

This covenantal name, "*The Lord our righteousness*" (Jeremiah 23:6), like all the other covenantal names in the Old Testament, points ultimately to Jesus and to the cross. That is where the exchange took place. That is where it became possible for Him to become our righteousness. After He had atoned for the sins of those who had failed to observe the law, He was made available to us as our righteousness. A Person is our righteousness; it is the Lord who is our righteousness.

A Restored Relationship with God

Israel's restoration to God's favor is also pictured as the restoration of a marriage relationship. It is as though Israel, through the covenant made at Sinai, had been married to Jehovah, or Yahweh. But then, Israel's unfaithfulness and idolatry broke that marriage relationship. That is why restoration is pictured in terms of a restored marriage relationship.

We find this concept in many of the books of the prophets. We will look at a few passages and then bring out a beautiful truth as a result. The Lord said to Israel,

> *I will betroth you to Me forever; yes, I will betroth you to Me in righteousness and in justice, in lovingkindness and in compassion, and I will betroth you to Me in faithfulness. Then you will know the Lord.* (Hosea 2:19–20)

The word "*betroth*" indicates the restoration of the marriage relationship between the Lord and His people. Next, let's look at this passage in Isaiah:

> *I will rejoice greatly in the Lord, my soul will exult in my God; for He has clothed me with garments of salvation, He has wrapped me with a robe of righteousness* [a robe of righteousness covers us completely], *as a bridegroom decks himself with a garland, and as a bride adorns herself with her jewels.* (Isaiah 61:10)

Then, a little further on in Isaiah, we find a promise to Israel's land and to Israel as a people.

> *It will no longer be said to you, "Forsaken," nor to your land will it any longer be said, "Desolate"; but you will be called, "My delight is in her," and your land, "Married"; for the LORD delights in you, and to Him your land will be married. For as a young man marries a virgin, so your sons will marry you; and as the bridegroom rejoices over the bride, so your God will rejoice over you.* (Isaiah 62:4–5)

We see that the restoration of righteousness brings the restoration of the marriage relationship. The Lord can be married once more to His people because their sins have been atoned for and they are clothed with the robe of His righteousness.

Taking His Name

This restoration was brought out in a very beautiful way by the prophet Jeremiah. At the beginning of this chapter, we looked at the passage in Jeremiah 23 that says, "*This is His name by which He* [the Lord] *will be called, 'The Lord our righteousness'*" (verse 6). Now, let's look at Jeremiah 33 to see the corresponding passage:

> *In those days and at that time I will cause a righteous Branch of David* [the Messiah] *to spring forth; and He shall execute justice and righteousness on the earth. In those days Judah shall be saved, and Jerusalem shall dwell in safety; and this is the name by which she shall be called: the LORD is our righteousness.* (Jeremiah 33:15–16)

That is a beautiful picture! Can you see the meaning of it?

First, "*this is the name by which **she** shall be called: the LORD is our righteousness.*" He is our righteousness. Yet when He takes His people back to Himself in righteousness, and when His people again become His bride, then, just as in human marriage custom, the bride takes the name of the bridegroom.

We are identified with Him. He Himself becomes our righteousness.

When we are united to Him, then our name also becomes "*The LORD our righteousness.*" We are clothed with His righteousness. We are identified with Him. He Himself becomes our righteousness. We are no longer dependent on our own efforts or struggles. We are no longer held back by our failures and our sins.

We have moved into a new relationship with God, a person-to-person relationship in which the Lord Himself is our righteousness. We are so identified with Him that, as a bride bears the bridegroom's name, so we bear His name—"*The LORD our righteousness.*"

9

The One Who Is There

We now come to the seventh and last of the covenantal names of Jehovah, *The One Who Is There* (*Permanently Present* or *Ever Present*). This name is found in the last verse of the book of Ezekiel:

> And the name of the city from that day shall be, "The LORD [*Jehovah*] is there." (Ezekiel 48:35)

The last nine chapters of Ezekiel are connected with the restoration of Israel, and they describe both the rebuilding of a city and the building of a temple.

Tremendous details are given to us about the construction of the temple, the materials that are used, the dimensions, and so on. Then, when the temple and the city are complete, God's name is given to it: "*The LORD is there*." This name brings out, of course, the real purpose for building both the city and the temple—that they should be a dwelling place for the Lord. It is as though the Lord waits until everything is complete and exactly the way He wants it. Then, He says, "Now, this is going to be My dwelling place. I'm going to be there."

The Shekinah Presence

We should look for a moment at the background to this whole situation. One major theme of Ezekiel is the glory of the Lord,

> ### *God's glory is His manifest presence among His people.*

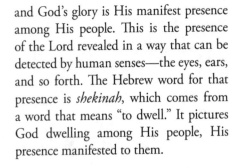

and God's glory is His manifest presence among His people. This is the presence of the Lord revealed in a way that can be detected by human senses—the eyes, ears, and so forth. The Hebrew word for that presence is *shekinah*, which comes from a word that means "to dwell." It pictures God dwelling among His people, His presence manifested to them.

The Withdrawal of God's Presence

At the opening of the prophecy of Ezekiel, God's glory was still in the temple in Jerusalem. But because of Israel's continuing sin and rebelliousness, God had to withdraw His personal presence. His glory departed from the temple and from the city. This is described as Ezekiel saw it himself:

> *Then the cherubim lifted up their wings with the wheels beside them, and the glory of the God of Israel hovered over them. And the glory of the LORD went up from the midst of the city, and stood over the mountain* [the Mount of Olives] *which is east of the city.* (Ezekiel 11:22–23)

At this point, God was so grieved by the sin of His people that He withdrew His presence from the temple and from the city. The glory of the Lord went out from the midst of the city, went away eastward, and hovered for a while over the Mount of Olives, to the east of the city. After the withdrawal of the Lord's glory, terrible judgments are predicted in the prophecies that follow. But, always interspersed with these judgments are the promises of restoration.

The Restoration of God's Presence

Then, we come to the closing chapters of Ezekiel, which are the description of restoration. The focus—the center, the most important part—of all the restoration is the restoration of the glory of the Lord, the shekinah, to the temple. It is described in Ezekiel 43:

Then he led me to the gate, the gate facing toward the east [east was the way in which the glory of the Lord had departed]; *and behold, the glory of the God of Israel was coming from the way of the east* [He was now returning from the same direction in which He had departed]. *And His voice was like the sound of many waters; and the earth shone with His glory. And it was like the appearance of the vision which I saw, like the vision which I saw when He came to destroy the city. And the visions were like the vision which I saw by the river Chebar; and I fell on my face. And the glory of the* LORD *came into the house by the way of the gate facing toward the east. And the Spirit lifted me up and brought me into the inner court; and behold, the glory of the* LORD *filled the house.*

(Ezekiel 43:1–5)

The Lord had come right back into the inner court of the house.

Then I heard one speaking to me from the house, while a man was standing beside me. And He said to me, "Son of man, this is the place of My throne and the place of the soles of My feet, where I will dwell among the sons of Israel forever."

(verses 6–7)

The essence of these passages is the return of the visible, manifest presence of the Lord to dwell again with His people forever. They bring out the ultimate purpose of God in His dealings with man.

God's Ultimate Purpose: Heaven on Earth

Very often, we have the wrong impression of God's purpose. We think His ultimate purpose is somehow to get man to heaven. But that really isn't it. God's purpose is to bring heaven down to man and, above all, to bring His own personal presence to man.

This was the purpose of every structure on earth the Lord caused to be built for Him. It was the purpose of the tabernacle of Moses. It was the purpose of the temple of Solomon. Always, these structures were to be dwelling places where God could reside in the midst of His people and never have to leave them.

But, alas, in the course of the history of God's people up until this time, they had behaved in such a way that the Lord had to withdraw His glory. However, the Lord persists in His purpose. Let's move forward to the end of the Bible, where we see that this purpose remains unchanged:

> *And I saw a new heaven and a new earth; for the first heaven and the first earth passed away, and there is no longer any sea. And I saw the holy city, new Jerusalem, coming down out of heaven from God, made ready as a bride adorned for her husband. And I heard a loud voice from the throne, saying, "Behold, the tabernacle of God is among men, and He shall dwell among them, and they shall be His people, and God Himself shall be among them."* (Revelation 21:1–3)

That is the climax—the outworking of the divine purpose of God in human history. Not that God would get man up to heaven, but that God would so deal with man as to make him fit to receive God's presence as a dwelling place on earth.

We return now to the climax of God's purpose as revealed at the close of Ezekiel:

> *The name of the city from that day shall be, "The* LORD *is there."* (Ezekiel 48:35)

That is the consummation of divine purpose.

The Seven Covenantal Names of God

Let's now review the seven covenantal names of Jehovah, or Yahweh, in their completeness and meditate on what each one means. I think you will find it a blessing to memorize these in order:

1. The One Who Provides
2. The One Who Heals

3. The One Who Is Our Banner

4. The One Who Is Our Peace

5. The One Who Is Our Shepherd

6. The One Who Is Our Righteousness

7. The One Who Is There (Permanently Present)

Again, God's ultimate purpose is to dwell forever with His people, and His purpose for each one of us individually is that we should know Him as a permanent, indwelling Lord—the Lord who is always there, right in the midst of our hearts and lives.

I wonder if you know the Lord in this way. Have you ever invited the Lord to make His dwelling in your heart and in your life? God wants you to do that. Jesus said in Revelation 3:20,

> *Behold, I stand at the door and knock; if anyone hears My voice and opens the door, I will come in to him, and will dine with him, and he with Me.*

The Lord's desire, His purpose, is to come into you—to make your heart and life His home, His permanent dwelling place. In all His covenantal fullness, in every one of those aspects of His covenantal nature, He wants to come in and dwell in your heart and life. The Lord is a gentleman, however. He will not push His way in. It is up to you to open the door. You have to invite Him in through faith in the sacrifice of God the Son—Christ Jesus—for you.

The Lord's desire, His purpose, is to make your heart and life His permanent dwelling place.

If you would like to do that right now, here is a brief prayer you can say:

> Lord Jesus Christ, I thank You that You died on the cross for my sins and that You rose from the dead. I invite You now to come in and dwell in my heart and be my Savior and my Lord. Amen.

Now, begin to thank Him. He was just waiting for the opportunity to come in. The moment you opened the door, He came in, and your life is going to be different from now on. This great, wonderful, covenant-keeping God is not someone you just hear about. He is someone who is forever there with you.

GOD'S "DISGUISES"

Introduction to Section 2

Why Does God Use "Disguises"?

We have seen that, in the Bible, names are indicative of the nature of the person named—they make known something about that person's character and destiny. Likewise, God's names, titles, and manifestations, as revealed to humanity in Scripture, indicate His nature and purposes. Yet, sometimes, God uses "disguises" when He interacts with human beings.

Why should God want to use "disguises"? Surely, we think He would be the last One to do such a thing. Yet the principle that God sometimes uses concealment is stated in various places in Scripture. Particularly, there is this thought-provoking verse:

> *It is the glory of God to conceal a matter, but the glory of kings is to search out a matter.* (Proverbs 25:2)

We see here that it rests with God to conceal and with kings to search out. In a certain way, the word *kings* represents the highest level of humanity. So, we can conclude that one of the highest achievements of humanity on its highest level is to search out what God has concealed. In this section of *Power in the Name*, therefore, we will be exploring why and how God comes to us in forms that have to be searched out.

To begin with, there are three things God does *not* want to do when He comes to you and me.

God Does Not Want To...

Overawe Us with His Power

First, God does not want to overawe us with His power. Although He will confirm the truth of the gospel and draw people to Himself through His power (see, for example, Romans 15:18–19; Hebrews 2:3–4), He does not want us to receive Him merely because He is all-powerful. In other words, we need not be afraid that if we do not receive Him, He will crush us in an instant—take away our breath and end our lives. That is not a motive pleasing to God for us to receive Him. Rather, our motive should be love:

> *In this is love, not that we loved God, but that He loved us and sent His Son to be the propitiation for our sins....And we have come to know and have believed the love which God has for us. God is love, and the one who abides in love abides in God, and God abides in him. By this, love is perfected with us, that we may have confidence in the day of judgment; because as He is, so also are we in this world. There is no fear in love; but perfect love casts out fear, because fear involves punishment, and the one who fears is not perfected in love. We love, because He first loved us.*
> (1 John 4:10, 16–19)

Entice Us through Blessings

Second, God does not want to entice us with His blessings. God is able to bless us in every area of our lives. He is able to give us all we need and much more. He is able to heal us, provide us with financial abundance, and solve all our problems. But He does not want us to receive Him merely on the basis of what we get from Him.

Satisfy Merely Our Intellectual Curiosity

Third, God does not want to satisfy mere intellectual curiosity. For some people, life is like a jigsaw puzzle made up of many different pieces, one of which is labeled *God*. Some people want to be able to insert God in His "rightful" place in the puzzle. But God is not just a piece in a puzzle. And if we have that attitude toward Him, He will not reveal Himself to us.

I have heard people say, "If I can put God in a test tube, I'll believe in Him." That is ridiculous! Any god that can be put into a test tube is not a god worth believing in.

Let me just restate what God does not want to do when He comes to us: (1) He does not want to overawe us with His power, (2) He does not want to entice us with His blessings, and (3) He does not want to satisfy mere intellectual curiosity.

What, then, does God want? I think we can put it this way: God wants us to desire Him for Himself—apart from His power, His blessings, and any other benefit.

God wants us to desire Him for Himself—apart from His power, His blessings, and any other benefit.

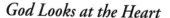

God Looks at the Heart

We need to realize that God does not look at us as we look at one another. He looks right down into the innermost depths of our hearts. A verse in 1 Samuel makes this point clearly and vividly. The prophet Samuel had been sent to the house of Jesse to anoint one of Jesse's sons to be the next king of Israel. Jesse presented the first of his sons, Eliab, and Samuel was impressed. But God said, *"Do not look at his appearance or at the height of his stature, because I have rejected him"* (1 Samuel 16:7).

Jesse produced seven of his fine, upstanding, handsome sons and presented them to Samuel, saying, "Which is to be the king?" Samuel was impressed by each one of them. Yet every time he was impressed by the outward appearance, God said, in effect, "That isn't the one."

After Samuel had run through all the sons whom Jesse presented and still there was no king, Samuel asked, "Isn't there anyone else?" Rather reluctantly, Jesse said, "There's one more, the youngest, but he's out in the pastures looking after the sheep." As it turned out, that eighth son—the one they had disregarded—was David, the future king of Israel. And when he arrived, the Lord said, "This is the one. Anoint him."

Then, the Lord spoke these words to Samuel:

For God sees not as man sees, for man looks at the outward appearance, but the LORD looks at the heart.   (1 Samuel 16:7)

God does not look at our outward appearances; He looks at our hearts. At the same time, the Lord does not want us to regard Him merely by outward appearance or external attributes. God wants us to receive Him for Himself, without regard to His tremendous qualities of power, riches, or wisdom.

Somehow, in His tremendous humility, God does not want to be wanted for what we can get from Him; rather, He wants to be wanted for Himself. He arranges situations and circumstances in the lives of every one of us that will sooner or later put us to this test: are we seeking God and believing in Him because of what we get or because of God Himself?

God Is Looking for People Who Are...

What does God look for in our hearts? To answer this question, I am going to give you a series of requirements from three passages in the Old Testament. Two passages come from the book of Psalms and one comes from the book of Isaiah. I believe these passages state very clearly and consistently what God really looks for in us.

"Broken and Crushed"

Let us look at the first requirement:

The LORD is near to the brokenhearted, and saves those who are crushed in spirit.   (Psalm 34:18)

An alternative reading for "*crushed in spirit*" is *contrite*. Actually, by its root from the Latin, *contrite* means just that—somebody who has been crushed, squashed down, battered. We use the word *broken* in modern speech in just the same way.

God is looking for those who are broken and crushed. Doesn't that seem strange?

Humble in Heart

Here is the second passage, and the second requirement:

> *Though the LORD is on high, he looks upon the lowly, but the proud he knows from afar.* (Psalm 138:6 NIV)

God looks for the lowly, but He knows the proud from afar. If you ask my opinion, that is where He keeps them—far off. Proud people really do not have access to God.

Contrite in Spirit

Third, we find a most beautiful passage in Isaiah. It describes God's eternal glory and majesty—and also what He looks for in us:

> *For this is what the high and lofty One says—he who lives forever* ["who inhabits eternity" NKJV], *whose name is holy: "I live in a high and holy place* [Isn't that awesome and impressive?], *but also with him who is contrite and lowly in spirit, to revive the spirit of the lowly and to revive the heart of the contrite."* (Isaiah 57:15 NIV)

Even though God is high and majestic, and even though He inhabits eternity (His dwelling place), He has one other dwelling place of choice. He lives also with him who is contrite and lowly in spirit.

In this passage, we see clearly that God is looking for the contrite and the lowly—those who are not proud, arrogant, self-confident, or self-reliant. Instead, these are people who, in many cases, have passed through some kind of experience in life that has stripped them of self-confidence and arrogance. This experience has left them—in the true meaning of the word—*broken*. That is what God is looking for: the lowly, the contrite, the broken.

—— ☙ ——

Contrite means being genuinely sorry for wrongdoing.

—— ☙ ——

Contrite means being genuinely sorry for wrongdoing. You see, lots of people do wrong and suffer unpleasant consequences. Although they want to get out of the consequences, they are not truly sorry for the wrongdoing. God does not really want to consider those people. He wants to engage with people who not only want to get out of the consequences, but also are sorry for the wrongdoing that brought them to those consequences.

Recognize God's Innermost Nature

In the next several chapters, we will see more clearly how God comes to us in disguises. He comes to us in such a way that if we are not sensitive enough to look for what God is in His innermost nature, we will not recognize Him. If we are concerned only with externals or with our own selfish ends, purposes, and desires, we will miss Him.

That is why God comes to humanity in disguises. And that is why it is so important that we learn to recognize those disguises. Otherwise, God may come to us and we may miss Him.

10

The Carpenter's Son

The first disguise we will examine is also the most important and marvelous disguise in which God ever came upon the stage of human history. He came to us in the disguise of the carpenter's son, known in history as Jesus of Nazareth.

Through prophecy, God warned Israel in advance that He was going to come to them in a strange way.

> *For a child will be born to us, a son will be given to us; and the government will rest on His shoulders; and His name will be called Wonderful Counselor, Mighty God, Eternal Father, Prince of Peace.* (Isaiah 9:6)

Isn't it remarkable that this "*child*" in Scripture is actually called "*Mighty God*"? Who could that be but Jesus?

The Scripture is so accurate. It says two things about this child. First, it says He will be "*born*" as a child but "*given*" as a son. Jesus did not become the Son of God through His incarnation. Eternally, He is the Son of God. He was the Son who was given, but through the incarnation, He became the little child.

**Eternally,
Jesus is the
Son of God.**

Seven Marvelous Facts about God's Son

Jesus' eternal nature is described elsewhere in the Bible. Let's read, for instance, a passage from the book of Hebrews:

> *In the past God spoke to our forefathers through the prophets at many times and in various ways, but in these last days he has spoken to us by his Son, whom he appointed heir of all things, and through whom he made the universe. The Son is the radiance of God's glory and the exact representation of his being, sustaining all things by his powerful word. After he had provided purification for sins, he sat down at the right hand of the Majesty in heaven.* (Hebrews 1:1–3 NIV)

This passage tells us seven marvelous facts about the Son of God.

First, He is heir of all. The entire creation, the entire universe, is going to find its consummation and fulfillment in Him.

Second, through Him, God the Father made the universe. He is the creative source of all.

Third, He is the radiance of God the Father's glory. He is the expression of what cannot be seen of the invisible God. He is the way God's glory comes into our lives.

Fourth, He is the exact representation of God the Father's being. He conveys to us, in a form we can appreciate, the exact nature of the eternal, invisible God. Jesus said, *"Anyone who has seen me has seen the Father"* (John 14:9 NIV).

Fifth, He sustains all things by His powerful word. He is the upholding force in the entire universe. (He is the one who upholds all creation.)

Sixth, He provided purification for our sins through His death on the cross.

Seventh, having done His work on the cross, He sat down at God's right hand, at the place of all authority, power, and glory in the universe.

Those seven facts reveal who Jesus really is. But, in history, He came to us in that strange disguise—the little baby who grew up to be the carpenter's son.

The Danger of Missing God

God warned Israel that they were in danger of missing Him. For instance, there is a well-known passage in Isaiah 53 that describes Jesus as the "man of sorrows." This passage begins with a warning about unbelief:

> *Who has believed our message and to whom has the arm of the LORD been revealed?* (verse 1 NIV)

"The arm of the Lord" is none other than Jesus. The passage describes Him in His human form:

> *He grew up before him like a tender shoot, and like a root out of dry ground.* (verse 2 NIV)

Israel was dry ground when Jesus came—that is, in spiritual dearth and need.

> *He had no beauty or majesty to attract us to him, nothing in his appearance that we should desire him.* (verse 2 NIV)

Again, God doesn't want to be desired for His outward appearance.

> *He was despised and rejected by men, a man of sorrows, and familiar with suffering. Like one from whom men hide their faces he was despised, and we esteemed him not. Surely he took up our infirmities and carried our sorrows, yet we considered him stricken by God, smitten by him, and afflicted. But he was pierced for our transgressions, he was crushed for our iniquities; the punishment that brought us peace was upon him, and by his wounds we are healed.* (verses 3–5 NIV)

His role as the bearer of the sins of the world was the greatest of all God's disguises.

Picture that mutilated, mangled, beaten form on the cross. Picture Him dying there, gasping out His life in agony, pouring out His lifeblood. Wasn't that a strange disguise for almighty God?

The Scripture goes on to say,

> We all, like sheep, have gone astray, each of us has turned to his own way; and the LORD has laid on him the iniquity of us all. (Isaiah 53:6 NIV)

His role as the bearer of the sins of the world was the greatest and the strangest of all God's disguises.

What the Son of God Was Not

Let us look at four things that the Son of God was not as He came to us in human form. He was not from the ruling priestly caste. He was not highly educated. He was not a political leader. He was not a military commander.

These are all roles that the world would have looked for in the Messiah. Those traits would have caused the world to admire, respect, and receive Him. But He had none of them. Why? Because God did not want to be received on that basis. He wanted to be received only by those whose hearts were lowly and contrite—those who were longing for God for Himself and not for what He had to offer.

True, Jesus was from the kingly tribe, the only tribe from which a king could ever come to the Jewish people. He was of the tribe of Judah. But its glory had long been eclipsed. And when Jesus came, He was just a *"root out of dry ground"* (Isaiah 53:2 NIV). That is how God came to humanity more than two thousand years ago. How few have penetrated the depths of that disguise.

Opposite Reactions to Jesus

When God came to earth in the disguise of the Man Jesus, whose life ended on a cross, people had opposite reactions to Him. One attitude dismissed Him with contempt as the carpenter's son. The other received Him with worship as the Son of God. Let's take a closer look at these divergent reactions.

The first reaction, one of rejection and contempt, is described in Matthew 13. Appropriately enough, in an unmistakable way, it describes the response to Jesus from those in His own hometown of Nazareth.

> *Coming to his hometown, he began teaching the people in their synagogue, and they were amazed. "Where did this man get this wisdom and these miraculous powers?" they asked. "Isn't this the carpenter's son? Isn't his mother's name Mary, and aren't his brothers James, Joseph, Simon and Judas? Aren't all his sisters with us? Where then did this man get all these things?" And they took offense at him. But Jesus said to them, "Only in his hometown and in his own house is a prophet without honor."* (Matthew 13:54–57 NIV)

These people could not see through the disguise. They had known Jesus too long. In a certain sense, they had been too familiar with Him. There is a saying that "familiarity breeds contempt," and I think, in large part, that was true in this case. The people who, in a sense, had been closest to Him failed to figure out the disguise. He had to go elsewhere to be received.

Let us look now at the opposite reaction. Those who received Him recognized the disguise and realized who He really was.

> *When Jesus came to the region of Caesarea Philippi, he asked his disciples, "Who do people say the Son of Man is?" They replied, "Some say John the Baptist; others say Elijah; and still others, Jeremiah or one of the prophets." "But what about you?" he asked. "Who do you say I am?" Simon Peter answered,*

> *"You are the Christ* [Messiah], *the Son of the living God." Jesus replied, "Blessed are you, Simon son of Jonah, for this was not revealed to you by man, but by my Father in heaven."*
> (Matthew 16:13–17 NIV)

Here was a man who received the revelation of the Father concerning Jesus—a man who looked beyond the superficialities, beyond what was not really important. By the grace of God and the Spirit of God, Peter discerned the true, eternal Son of God, the Messiah, the One for whom the Israelites had been waiting, but whom they failed as a whole to recognize.

How Will You Respond to Jesus?

We still have those two alternatives today. We can react in one way or the other, just as the Israelites could. We need to be mindful of these words from the first chapter of John's gospel:

> *He came to His own, and those who were His own did not receive Him. But as many as received Him, to them He gave the right to become children of God, even to those who believe in His name, who were born not of blood, nor of the will of the flesh, nor of the will of man, but of God.*
> (John 1:11–13)

What are you going to do about Jesus? Are you going to reject Him? Or are you going to receive Him?

Are you going to look beneath the disguise and see the eternal Son of God? Are you going to worship Him and welcome Him in your life? I pray that you may do this.

11

Children

For God's second disguise, we will look at one that He regularly uses. Many times, God comes to us in the disguise of a child. Look at what Jesus said:

> *At that time the disciples came to Jesus and asked, "Who is the greatest in the kingdom of heaven?" He called a little child and had him stand among them. And he said: "I tell you the truth, unless you change and become like little children, you will never enter the kingdom of heaven. Therefore, whoever humbles himself like this child is the greatest in the kingdom of heaven. And whoever welcomes a little child like this in my name welcomes me. But if anyone causes one of these little ones who believe in me to sin, it would be better for him to have a large millstone hung around his neck and to be drowned in the depths of the sea."*
>
> (Matthew 18:1–6 NIV)

Then, a little further on, Jesus said,

> *See that you do not look down on one of these little ones. For I tell you that their angels in heaven always see the face of my Father in heaven.*
>
> (verse 10 NIV)

God Identifies Himself with Children

God sets great value upon children. In fact, as I understand the above Scripture, an angel is appointed to guard every child. This angel has direct access to the presence of almighty God and has to give God a report on what happens to that child. And Jesus said if God brings us into contact with a child, and we receive that child, we are receiving Jesus. But, if we reject that child—if we refuse to help that child—in reality, we are rejecting Jesus.

The Scripture also says it is worse yet for us if we do anything to cause such a little child to sin (and remember, our contemporary society is full of men and women who are doing this). According to Jesus, it would be better for such a person to have a large millstone hung around his neck and to be drowned in the depths of the sea than to incur the guilt of causing a child to sin.

We see from this Scripture that when Jesus sets a child before us, He identifies Himself with that child. Our response to the child parallels our response to Jesus. God's angel in heaven is watching over that child and watching how we respond to the little one.

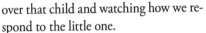

God often disguises Himself in the weak, the unimpressive, the improbable, the unconventional.

We come back to the same principle: God often disguises Himself in the weak, the unimpressive, the improbable, the unconventional. We cannot take it for granted that we will know when God comes into our lives. He will come in disguises, and unless our hearts are open, we will miss Him. We may be guilty of rejecting God without even knowing that He came to us.

Acceptable Religion

The principle is very clear throughout all of Scripture—in both the Old Testament and the New—that God requires us to care for children in need. James included this requirement when he listed a

number of evidences of true religion. Let's look at these evidences.
First, those with true religion keep tight reins on their tongues.

> *If anyone considers himself religious and yet does not keep a*
> *tight rein on his tongue, he deceives himself and his religion*
> *is worthless.* (James 1:26 NIV)

That one comment writes off much of contemporary religion.
If a person does not control his tongue, God will not accept his
religion. Those with "loose tongues" include gossips, slanderers, and
talebearers—people who exaggerate and people who criticize. God
does not accept their religion at all.

What kind of religion is God looking for?

> *Religion that God our Father accepts as pure and fault-*
> *less is this: to look after orphans and widows in their dis-*
> *tress and to keep oneself from being polluted by the world.*
> (verse 27 NIV)

There are two aspects to that kind of acceptable religion. One is
positive, the other is negative. The positive is stated first. It is to look
after orphans and widows in their distress. The negative is next. It is
to keep ourselves from being polluted by the world.

Unfortunately, it seems that much of contemporary Christianity
emphasizes only the negative—not being involved with the world,
not being polluted by the world. We hear
much about keeping ourselves separate,
not going here or there, not doing this
or that—much of which is often just human regulations.

People who emphasize such things
often totally miss the positive, the first
part, which is to look after orphans and
widows in their distress. The way we respond to children in need is the way we
respond to God.

The way we
respond to
children in need
is the way we
respond to God.

When Jesus Came to Me

I want to relate a personal experience in regard to this subject. My first wife, Lydia, and I raised a family of nine adopted girls. Six were Jewish, one was English, one was Arab, and the youngest was African. When I married my second wife, Ruth, she brought three adopted children into our family. Between us, we were responsible for twelve adopted children. So, what I relate next is not just theory—it represents a great amount of experience.

Here is a brief account of how Lydia and I received the little black African girl who became our ninth adopted daughter. Lydia and I were missionaries in Kenya, in east Africa, at the time, and we were very busy with educational work. One night, a white lady and a black couple came to our home with a little baby who was about six months old. The child was very sickly and was wrapped in nothing but a dirty towel. They said to us, "We've heard that you take in children." My wife and I replied, "Yes, that was true of us many years ago, but we're too old to do that now. And besides, we're too busy with other work." To that, these people replied, "We've been going around for three days to every family—white, black, Asian—looking for somebody to take this little child. We're so tired. Would you just let us sit down and rest for about half an hour?" So we said, "By all means, sit down." And we sat there with them.

At the end of half an hour, they got up to go. As they carried their baby past me, this little one just stretched out her hand toward me, as if to say, "What are you going to do about me?" I turned to my wife and said, "I think we'll change our minds." Lydia said to the couple, "Give me a week to get a baby crib and some baby clothes, and bring her back." So, that's how we took that little African girl.

I will tell you this: my life has been much richer for taking that little girl. Today, she is grown up; she is a beautiful Christian woman who is married and serving the Lord. I shudder to think what I could have missed if I had let that opportunity go by—when Jesus came to me in the person of that little sick baby.

What Will You Do?

Our world today is full of children in need. And those children are not just outside the United States. There are plenty in the U.S., as well. It is in our power, in many cases, to help them—either directly or indirectly.

For many years, I have systematically provided support for two orphans in India and one in Korea. I say this not to boast but to make a point. What is the good of preaching if we don't practice what we preach? It does not cost much, and I am keeping three children alive and giving them the opportunity to have a Christian education.

To close this chapter, let's examine those familiar words of James again:

Anyone, then, who knows the good he ought to do and doesn't do it, sins. (James 4:17 NIV)

Sin does not include just sins of commission—what we have done wrong. Many times, the sins we commit are sins of omission—what we have failed to do. If God comes to us in the person of a little child, what are we going to do about it?

12

God's Messengers

Another disguise God has used many times in history and continues to use today is His messengers. It is a principle in Scripture—one that is demonstrated many times and emphasized in scriptural teaching—that God identifies Himself with those whom He sends as His representatives. This means the way we respond to God's messengers is counted by God as our response to God Himself. We cannot reject God's messengers and claim to receive God. I am afraid some people simply have not grasped this concept.

God identifies Himself with those whom He sends as His representatives.

The Principle of Identification

Let's look at what Jesus said about this subject in some passages in the New Testament. The first passage is from the book of John. Jesus said to His disciples,

> *I tell you the truth, whoever accepts anyone I send accepts me; and whoever accepts me accepts the one who sent me.*
> (John 13:20 NIV)

In this verse, we see that the principle goes all the way down from God the Father. God the Father sent Jesus, His Son. Those who received Jesus received God the Father. Conversely, those who rejected Jesus rejected God the Father. (See John 12:48–50.)

But the principle does not end there. Jesus, in turn, chose certain men—and rather unlikely men. They were not theologians, they were not priests, and they were not highly educated. They were fishermen and tax collectors and such, people whom the world would not have esteemed very highly. Jesus made them His disciples and sent them out as His representatives. And He said, in effect, "The way people treat you is the way people treat Me. If they receive you, they receive Me; but if they reject you, they are rejecting Me [though they may not recognize it]. If they reject Me, they are also rejecting My Father." That is a very emphatic verse.

Acceptance or Rejection

Jesus stated this principle of identification—and of acceptance or rejection—more fully when He sent His first disciples out to preach the kingdom of God.

> *Whatever town or village you enter, search for some worthy person there and stay at his house until you leave. As you enter the home, give it your greeting. If the home is deserving, let your peace rest on it; if it is not, let your peace return to you.*
> (Matthew 10:11–13 NIV)

It is a remarkable fact that the messengers of Jesus have the authority and the ability to transmit His peace to those who receive them. But they can also withhold His peace from those who do not receive them in a worthy way. Jesus continued,

> *If anyone will not welcome you or listen to your words, shake the dust off your feet when you leave that home or town.*
> (verse 14 NIV)

To shake the dust off your feet was a sign of totally disowning something. To do so was to say, "I accept no responsibility for you."

Jesus continued His instruction to His disciples with this very remarkable statement about those who reject them:

> *I tell you the truth, it will be more bearable for Sodom and Gomorrah on the day of judgment than for that town.*
> (Matthew 10:15 NIV)

Sodom and Gomorrah were cities that were guilty of a sin that God utterly condemned and judged. God judged them with a remarkable, dramatic overthrow, setting them forth as an example to all who should indulge in that sin in future times. What Sodom and Gomorrah experienced was terrible! But Jesus said it will be worse for people who reject His messengers than it was for Sodom and Gomorrah! I hope it is becoming clear how serious it is that we do not reject the messengers whom Jesus sends.

Jesus continued His message to His disciples on their acceptance or rejection:

> *I am sending you out like sheep among wolves. Therefore be as shrewd as snakes and as innocent as doves.*
> (verse 16 NIV)

There is nothing very impressive about a sheep. Jesus could have used many other figures of speech. He could have said, "I'm sending you out like lions," or "like leopards," or "like horses." All these creatures have some kind of impressive feature. But a sheep has never impressed anybody. Nor has a sheep ever terrified anybody! Jesus said, "That's how I'm going to send you. You'll be in the midst of wolves, but you'll be like sheep."

At the end of this chapter, Jesus said,

> *He who receives you receives me, and he who receives me receives the one who sent me.*
> (verse 40 NIV)

We see the same principle again: "If they receive you, they're receiving Me. If they receive Me, they're receiving the Father who sent Me. But, if they reject you, they're rejecting Me. If they're rejecting Me, they're also rejecting the Father."

Receiving God's Messengers Brings Reward

Jesus wrapped up His teaching on acceptance or rejection with an added emphasis, which is also a kind of principle:

> *Anyone who receives a prophet because he is a prophet will receive a prophet's reward, and anyone who receives a righteous man because he is a righteous man will receive a righteous man's reward.* (Matthew 10:41 NIV)

We know from the Bible that many of God's prophets were pretty strange people. They wore strange clothes, did strange things, turned up at unexpected moments, and made the most unwelcome statements. Sometimes, they just walked off the stage after that. You probably could not find a less conventional character than the prophet Elijah anywhere in literature!

If you identify a righteous man and receive him, you will receive the same reward as that righteous man.

But Jesus said it pays to discern the prophet beneath that unconventional or even unacceptable exterior. The reason? If you identify the prophet and receive him, you will receive the same reward as the prophet. If you identify a righteous man and receive him, you will receive the same reward as that righteous man.

God comes to us in the form of His messengers. He identifies Himself with the ones whom He sends to represent Him. And the way we receive them or reject them is counted as the way we receive or reject God Himself. Remember that to reject the messengers of Jesus is a worse sin than that of Sodom and Gomorrah.

Examples of God's Messengers

Barak the Judge

Let's look now at two rather interesting examples. The first is from the Old Testament—the example of Barak, one of the judges of Israel. In the time of Barak, Israel had been invaded and was being oppressed by an alien army more numerous, more powerful, and much better equipped and armed than Israel. In that context, God called on a young man named Barak, who was apparently not a very well-known figure, to lead Israel to victory against this invading army.

Barak was a rather retiring young man, and he did not feel qualified for the task at hand. So, he went to the prophetess of that day, whose name was Deborah, and asked her to go with him.

It's clear that Barak really was not a very impressive figure. Nevertheless, he was courageous and obedient. He led Israel's army to victory, and the alien army was defeated and driven out.

After that, Deborah the prophetess sang a song about the victory, celebrating it and speaking about various tribes in Israel. Some had come to help Barak, while others had refused. She spoke in particular about one village that is not mentioned again anywhere in the Scriptures, the village of Meroz. This is what she said about Meroz in her song:

> *"Curse Meroz," said the angel of the LORD. "Curse its people bitterly, because they did not come to help the LORD, to help the LORD against the mighty."*　　(Judges 5:23 NIV)

The people of Meroz thought they didn't need to help Barak, so they dismissed him. Perhaps they ridiculed him. But God didn't consider their indifferent response as committed against Barak. He regarded it as committed against Himself. A curse came upon that village because its people had not come to help Barak. And by failing to help Barak, they had failed to help the Lord Himself.

John the Baptist

The second example is John the Baptist. John was the forerunner, the representative, sent before Jesus to prepare His way. But Herod the Tetrarch did not like John because John questioned his morality, so he had John imprisoned. Then, one night, when a dancing girl came and pleased him (probably with some kind of sensual dance), Herod vowed that he would give her anything she asked for.

She was the daughter of the woman whom Herod had unlawfully married, and to get revenge on John the Baptist, this girl asked for his head. In order to keep his oath, Herod had John executed, and his head was brought on a plate right then and there. (See, for example, Mark 6:17–28.)

Later on, just after Jesus was arrested, He was brought before Herod to be tried:

> *When Herod saw Jesus, he was greatly pleased, because for a long time he had been wanting to see him. From what he had heard about him, he hoped to see him perform some miracle. He plied him with many questions, but Jesus gave him no answer*
> (Luke 23:8–9 NIV)

Herod had rejected John the Baptist, and he couldn't get any answer from Jesus. The principle is, if you reject God's servants and messengers, you cannot expect to hear from God.

13

God's Persecuted People

The last disguise we are going to look at—one that God has often used and still uses today—is His persecuted people. God suffers with His persecuted people, and He identifies Himself with them. The way we treat them is reckoned as the way we treat God Himself.

Saul Unknowingly Persecuted Christ

This principle is brought out so clearly in the example of Saul of Tarsus. When Saul is introduced in the New Testament, he is the number one persecutor of that strange new sect in Jerusalem that came to be known as "the Nazarenes." He was focusing his attack on the people who followed "the Way," those whom, today, we would identify as Christians.

Not content with persecuting the Christians in Jerusalem, Saul decided that he was going to stamp out this sect in every city. So, he obtained authority from the chief priest in Jerusalem to go to the city of Damascus and there arrest and deal with any followers of Jesus he might find there.

However, as Saul was on the way from Jerusalem to Damascus, he had an unexpected encounter with Jesus Himself. This is the description of the encounter, and I want you to note particularly the way in which Jesus spoke to Saul of Tarsus. (Of course, Saul later became the great apostle Paul.)

> *Meanwhile, Saul was still breathing out murderous threats against the Lord's disciples. He went to the high priest and asked him for letters to the synagogues in Damascus, so that if he found any there who belonged to the Way [Christians], whether men or women, he might take them as prisoners to Jerusalem. As he neared Damascus on his journey, suddenly a light from heaven flashed around him. He fell to the ground and heard a voice say to him, "Saul, Saul, why do you persecute me?" "Who are you, Lord?" Saul asked. "I am Jesus, whom you are persecuting," he replied. "Now get up and go into the city, and you will be told what you must do."*
>
> (Acts 9:1–6 NIV)

> *Jesus' question was not, "Why are you persecuting My people?" He asked, "Why are you persecuting Me?"*

Notice what Jesus asked Saul. His question was not, "Why are you persecuting My people?" or "…My followers?" or "…My disciples?" He asked, "Why are you persecuting Me?" When Saul asked who He was, the Lord replied, "*I am Jesus, whom you are persecuting.*"

God's people do not suffer alone. They may be persecuted terribly, but God is always with them in their sufferings. He is identified with them if they are persecuted for His name, for His glory, and in obedience to Him.

So, again, the way we treat God's persecuted people is regarded by God as the way we treat Him. Many rulers and leaders of society throughout the ages did not understand this. They persecuted the humble, poor people of God and didn't realize that they were actually dealing with God Himself in His people. We need to understand that Jesus identifies Himself with His persecuted people.

Make Sure You Are on God's Side

It is particularly important to understand this truth as this age draws to its close. The reason? Jesus Himself warned His followers that in the last days, there will be worldwide persecution of Christians, the followers of Jesus. This is what the Lord said in Matthew 24:

> *Jesus answered: "Watch out that no one deceives you. For many will come in my name, claiming, 'I am the Christ* [Messiah],' *and will deceive many. You will hear of wars and rumors of wars, but see to it that you are not alarmed. Such things must happen, but the end is still to come. Nation will rise against nation, and kingdom against kingdom. There will be famines and earthquakes in various places. All these are the beginning of birth pains."* (Matthew 24:4–8 NIV)

All around the world today, we are seeing what Jesus described in these verses. Those occurrences are the "birth pains" of a new age. The Lord added, in reference to this period,

> *Then you* [His disciples] *will be handed over to be persecuted and put to death, and you will be hated by all nations because of me.* (verse 9 NIV)

Again, there is going to be worldwide persecution of the followers of Jesus. Let's be on our guard that we never take the wrong side. Let's be careful never to allow ourselves to become identified in any way with the persecutors of the people of Jesus. If we do, we are going to have to answer to God as if we had treated God Himself that way.

Showing Mercy Qualifies Us for Mercy

On a more positive note, we can be among those who receive the people of God and show mercy to them. If we do so, we will, in turn, qualify for God's mercy. Let's refer to the passage of Scripture in Matthew that we noted earlier:

> *Anyone who receives a prophet because he is a prophet will receive a prophet's reward, and anyone who receives a righteous*

man because he is a righteous man will receive a righteous man's reward. (Matthew 10:41 NIV)

This passage talks about our ability to penetrate the disguise—to see who it is we are dealing with and to accept him for what he is in God and for how God sees him. When that happens, we qualify for the same reward as that person. If the person is a prophet, we qualify for a prophet's reward. If the person is a righteous man, we qualify for a righteous man's reward.

What Jesus said next comes down to some very basic responses:

If anyone gives even a cup of cold water to one of these little ones because he is my disciple, I tell you the truth, he will certainly not lose his reward. (verse 42 NIV)

> *We are going to be judged for the way we deal with God's people, especially when they are being persecuted.*

In other words, we are going to be judged by God for the way we deal with God's people, especially when they are being persecuted. Especially when they are in need. Especially when it would be easy to turn our backs on them.

We could say, "It's their fault. They shouldn't have been so religious. They should have been more careful about how they spoke." There is going to be real pressure to turn against God's persecuted people as this age comes to its close. But remember, if we turn against them, we are turning against God Himself.

Honoring Our Jewish Brothers and Sisters

We have seen that Jesus identifies Himself with His people who are persecuted. I want to add an important emphasis: this includes those who are His brothers by natural birth—that is, the Jewish people.

In Revelation 5:5, Jesus is called "*the Lion of the tribe of Judah*" (NIV). In other words, He is eternally identified in a special way with Judah. (Judah is the name from which we get the words *Jew* and *Jewish*.) Jesus, in a certain sense, is eternally identified with the Jewish people. And the way we treat the Jewish people is going to be reckoned to us as the way we have treated their great Elder Brother, their King, whom most of them have not yet recognized—Jesus Himself.

Presently, we see Israel becoming more and more the focus of world leaders and governments. Every day, we read something in the paper or see something on the news about Israel. That tiny nation of just under six million people is the focus of world news and global attention. This is not an accident. God has arranged it because He is going to judge the nations by the way they relate to Israel.

Let's look at a rather lengthy passage from Matthew 25 to see how Jesus brought this out so clearly.

> When the Son of Man comes in his glory, and all the angels with him, he will sit on his throne in heavenly glory. All the nations will be gathered before him, and he will separate the people one from another as a shepherd separates the sheep from the goats. He will put the sheep on his right and the goats on his left. Then the King will say to those on his right [the sheep], "Come, you who are blessed by my Father; take your inheritance, the kingdom prepared for you since the creation of the world. For I was hungry and you gave me something to eat, I was thirsty and you gave me something to drink, I was a stranger and you invited me in, I needed clothes and you clothed me, I was sick and you looked after me, I was in prison and you came to visit me." Then the righteous will answer him, "Lord, when did we see you hungry and feed you, or thirsty and give you something to drink? When did we see you a stranger and invite you in, or needing clothes and clothe you? When did we see you sick or in prison and go to visit you?" The King will reply, "I tell you the truth, whatever you did for one of the least of these brothers of mine, you did for me." Then he will say to those on his left, "Depart from me, you who are cursed, into the eternal fire prepared for the devil and his angels. For I was hungry and you

> *gave me nothing to eat, I was thirsty and you gave me noth-*
> *ing to drink, I was a stranger and you did not invite me in,*
> *I needed clothes and you did not clothe me, I was sick and in*
> *prison and you did not look after me." They also will answer,*
> *"Lord, when did we see you hungry or thirsty or a stranger or*
> *needing clothes or sick or in prison, and did not help you?" He*
> *will reply, "I tell you the truth, whatever you did not do for one*
> *of the least of these, you did not do for me." Then they will go*
> *away to eternal punishment, but the righteous to eternal life.*
> (Matthew 25:31–46 NIV)

What we do for the brothers and sisters of Jesus, we do for Him. What we do not do for His brothers and sisters, we do not do for Him.

What were the grounds for punishment for those in the above passage? In effect, they had failed to recognize Jesus in His persecuted people. In persecuting and siding against those people, or in neglecting them, they had taken their stand against almighty God Himself.

This is a serious thought, whether we apply it to the disciples of Jesus or to the people of Jesus by natural birth—the Jewish people. Speaking concerning the Jewish people, the prophet Zechariah said, in one concise sentence,

> *Whoever touches you touches the apple of his* [God's] *eye.*
> (Zechariah 2:8 NIV)

Remember that warning when you speak about the Jewish people, when you think about them, when you express your attitude concerning them. When you touch them, you are touching the most sensitive part of God—the very apple of His eye. Let's be on our guard.

GOD'S ULTIMATE REVELATION: JESUS THE CHRIST

Introduction to Section 3

Jesus' Nature and Purposes

A special atmosphere—different from all other seasons of the year—is generated in countries where the Christmas season is publicly honored and celebrated. In my own life, I can remember how, when I was a young person (even though I was at that time an unbeliever and far from God), the Christmas season touched my heart with special emotions each year. They were emotions I could not explain—ones that I partly desired and partly feared.

Somehow, those emotions reminded me of a missing dimension in my life that I needed to make me a complete person. Sad to say, those emotions didn't last long into the New Year. Nevertheless, I never totally forgot them. They were always there somewhere in the background.

It is essential that we keep Christ at the center of Christmas. Without Christ, Christmas loses any real or permanent significance. Unfortunately, for many people in contemporary Western culture, this season is often associated with materialism, commercialism, and self-indulgence. Scripture has a very clear warning for us about this:

For the one who sows to his own flesh shall from the flesh reap corruption, but the one who sows to the Spirit shall from the Spirit reap eternal life.　　　　　　(Galatians 6:8)

109

In all our thoughts, words, and actions, even the way we spend our time and money, we are always sowing something we will get back, or "reap." Scripture says that we can sow to the flesh—to the carnal, to the material, to self—but we will reap only corruption, disappointment, and frustration. Yet if we sow to the Spirit of God, we will reap eternal life. We will have richer, fuller, and more abundant lives, the kind of lives Jesus came to bring us.

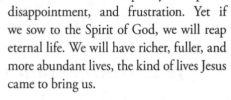

Sow to the Spirit by keeping your heart and mind focused on Jesus.

In order not to suffer the frustration of reaping from the flesh, we must sow to the Spirit. One special way to do this is to keep our hearts and minds focused on Jesus. The purpose of this section of the book, then, is to help us do this by deepening our understanding of Jesus' nature and purposes through an examination of ten of His titles.

14

Wonderful Counselor

As I stated earlier, we need to understand that in the Bible, names and titles are significant. Every biblical name has a specific meaning, and this applies, as well, to the names and titles of God. In addition, names often indicate something special about the character or destiny of the person to whom they are given.

This association applies particularly to the many titles given to Jesus. Each tells us something special and important about Him. Out of the many titles given to Jesus, I have chosen certain ones that, I believe, will especially bless you.

The first two titles we are going to look at come from the book of Isaiah:

> *For a child will be born to us, a son will be given to us; and the government will rest on His shoulders; and His name will be called Wonderful Counselor,…Prince of Peace.*
> (Isaiah 9:6)

In this chapter, we will focus on the title *Wonderful Counselor.* I would like to discuss the meaning of this title through another prophecy about the coming Messiah, also from the book of Isaiah:

> *Then a shoot will spring from the stem of Jesse, and a branch from his roots will bear fruit. And the Spirit of the LORD will rest on Him, the spirit of wisdom and understanding, the spirit of counsel and strength, the spirit of knowledge and the fear of the LORD.* (Isaiah 11:1–2)

In chapter 20, "Christ, or Messiah," I will explain further what the title *Messiah* means—"the anointed one." But here, we find the prediction of the Messiah, the One on whom the Spirit of the Lord will rest in His fullness. In particular, those aspects that make Him the Wonderful Counselor are emphasized here. The words we want to notice especially are *"wisdom," "understanding," "counsel,"* and *"knowledge."*

The One Who Has the Answers

I once heard a pastor preach a sermon in which he gave a description of Jesus I had never heard before—and it has stuck with me. He said, "Jesus, the Man with the plan." I say amen to that!

Jesus is the Counselor. He is the One who has the answer. He is the One who can show you what to do when nobody else can. Remember, when you have come to the end of your own wits and resources, there is a Wonderful Counselor.

In the Bible, wonderful always suggests something supernatural or marvelous.

Let me say a little about that word *wonderful*. It is used in various places in the Bible. *Wonderful* always suggests something supernatural or marvelous. So, in this picture of Jesus as the Wonderful Counselor, we see certain elements. First, His counsel is on a supernatural level. It is above mere psychology and human counseling, however helpful these things might be. Second, His counsel includes discernment. Jesus sees right to the heart of every problem and every person. Third, His counsel includes direction. He has the answer. Not only does He see the problem, but He also offers the solution.

Two Instances of Jesus as Counselor

Let us look at two illustrations in the Gospels of Jesus as the Wonderful Counselor. We will begin with one that involves the calling of His first disciples.

> As Jesus was walking beside the Sea of Galilee, he saw two brothers, Simon called Peter and his brother Andrew. They were casting a net into the lake, for they were fishermen. "Come, follow me," Jesus said, "and I will make you fishers of men." At once they left their nets and followed him.
> (Matthew 4:18–20 NIV)

From all the potential disciples, Jesus picked two men who were simple, plain fishermen. They had no great education, no association with priestly office or with teachers of the law. They were just fishermen. But Jesus, the Wonderful Counselor, saw something in those men. He knew what He could make out of them. So, He said, in essence, "If you'll commit yourselves to Me, if you'll follow Me, I'll make you fishers of men."

You need to understand that what is important in your relationship with Jesus is not what you are when you start but what He is going to make of you. His wonderful counsel sees in all those who come to Him what they can be if they yield to Him.

What is important in your relationship with Jesus is not what you are when you start but what He is going to make of you.

The second example is Jesus' encounter with the rich young ruler:

> As Jesus started on his way, a man ran up to him and fell on his knees before him. "Good teacher," he asked, "what must I do to

*inherit eternal life?" "Why do you call me good?" Jesus answered.
"No one is good—except God alone. You know the commandments: 'Do not murder, do not commit adultery, do not steal, do
not give false testimony, do not defraud, honor your father and
mother.'" "Teacher," he declared, "all these I have kept since I was
a boy." Jesus looked at him and loved him. "One thing you lack,"
he said. "Go, sell everything you have and give to the poor, and you
will have treasure in heaven. Then come, follow me." At this the
man's face fell. He went away sad, because he had great wealth.*
(Mark 10:17–22 NIV)

Jesus looked right into the heart of that young man. He loved him.
He wanted the best for him. But He had to tell him the truth.

The young ruler said, "I've kept all the commandments." Interestingly enough, the commandment not to covet is not mentioned
there. Jesus saw that there was just one barrier to what God had for
that young man, and that was his possessions. He was bound by the
material. Jesus looked right down into his heart and said, "There's
just one thing you have to do. Sell all you have and follow Me."

Jesus didn't say that to everybody, because He knew the particular hindrance in each life. But to this young man, He said, in effect,
"Money and possessions are your hindrance. If you want what I
have to offer, you'll have to let them go."

So, if you have a problem or a need, remember that there is a
Wonderful Counselor, Jesus. His office is open twenty-four hours a
day. Don't be afraid to go to Him.

15

Prince of Peace

As we have established, each of Jesus' titles tells us something special and important about Jesus Himself. Let us return to Isaiah 9:6, where we find a second title:

For a child will be born to us, a son will be given to us; and the government will rest on His shoulders; and His name will be called...Prince of Peace.

There is a certain emphasis on government in the above prophecy. It says, "*A child will be born..., a son will be given...; and the government will rest on His shoulders.*" The title in this verse that particularly emphasizes His character as a ruler is *Prince of Peace.*

We have to understand that the word *prince* in the Scriptures always designates a ruler. *Prince* is not just a title gained through family inheritance. It represents someone who is an active ruler, responsible for government. This is one feature brought out here in regard to the wonderful Child who was to come.

Peace Accompanies Righteous Government

Two things in our experience and in human history can never be separated from one another: the first is righteous government and the second is peace. This corollary is true of individuals, of nations, and even of whole civilizations. Only insofar as there is righteous government can there be peace.

We have a very limited and incomplete picture of peace in our contemporary society. We think there is peace as long as there isn't

open war. As long as nations are not actually fighting one another with military weapons, we say there is peace, but that is utterly ridiculous.

The Hebrew word for peace, shalom, implies "completeness" and contains the idea of order.

Whenever there is bitterness, hatred, slander, accusation, or systematic attempts to undermine other nations, outdo them, and bring them down, there is no peace. The Hebrew word for peace, *shalom*, implies much more than that. Its root meaning is "completeness," and it also contains the idea of order. True peace is order and completeness.

God's Government on Earth

The good news of the gospel is the establishment of God's righteous government, which is called "*His kingdom*" in the Scriptures. (See, for example, Matthew 6:33.) Many of us have missed this truth. Here is the good news: God is going to establish His righteous government through Jesus. Remember that the word *gospel* means "good news."

Let's look at the proclamation of the gospel as it is given in various passages in Matthew.

> *In those days John the Baptist came, preaching in the Desert of Judea and saying, "Repent, for the kingdom of heaven is near."*
> (Matthew 3:1–2 NIV)

John the Baptist was the first one to proclaim the gospel message. He said God's kingdom—His government—was coming. A little further on, we read the first recorded words Jesus preached publicly:

From that time on Jesus began to preach, "Repent, for the kingdom of heaven is near." (Matthew 4:17 NIV)

Jesus went throughout Galilee, teaching in their synagogues, preaching the good news of the kingdom, and healing every disease and sickness among the people. (verse 23 NIV)

Notice again that the good news is the kingdom—God's government coming to earth. And we are going to be able to enjoy the benefits of that government.

Later, in describing His program to bring this age to a close, Jesus said,

And this gospel [good news] *of the kingdom will be preached in the whole world as a testimony to all nations, and then the end will come.* (Matthew 24:14 NIV)

All nations have a right to hear—at least once—that God is going to set up His kingdom in the Person of Jesus, the Prince of Peace. That is the only hope for peace for humanity.

No Peace without the Prince of Peace

In Isaiah 57, we have God's promise of peace to all, but we also have a warning that peace is not for the wicked. Peace is not for those who refuse God's righteous government in the Person of Jesus. We cannot have peace apart from the Prince of Peace. This is what Isaiah says:

"Peace, peace to him who is far and to him who is near," says the LORD, "and I will heal him." (Isaiah 57:19)

That is God's offer of peace. Note, also, that peace and healing go together very closely. The passage continues,

But the wicked are like the tossing sea, for it cannot be quiet, and its waters toss up refuse and mud. "There is no peace," says my God, "for the wicked." (Isaiah 57:20–21)

Those who refuse God's government are like the sea that cannot rest. The sea is always tossing. It is never fully quiet; it cannot be totally calm. The elements of unrest and disturbance are always there, and these elements come through the rejection of God's righteous government in the Person of Jesus.

Jesus is the Prince of Peace, the only ruler whose government can bring peace to humanity.

Jesus Is the Answer for Nations

Let's consider how this truth applies to our contemporary situation. One of the most conspicuous features of the world condition today is the dearth of true leadership—mainly in the political realm, but in other areas, also. There seem to be just two alternatives offered to humanity. The first is dictatorial oppression, or totalitarianism. The second is weak, ineffectual leadership that doesn't really lead but merely follows where the multitude wants to go. Its decisions are often governed by the Harris or Gallup polls. That is not leadership.

People are faced, therefore, with two unwelcome choices. They are afraid of oppression, but they are tired of the confusion that results from ineffectual leadership. What is the solution? Actually, Jesus is the only solution. And humanity is being prepared to accept that solution. Humanity is being faced with the fact that there must be good government if there is to be peace. Humanity is also being confronted with the fact that man, in his own unregenerate, rebellious nature, cannot offer truly good government. So, God's answer is Jesus, the Prince of Peace.

Jesus Is the Answer for You

But, thank God, you don't have to wait until the future to experience the peace that Jesus brings. If you will willingly yield to the lordship of Jesus in your life, you can have that peace right now. Paul said,

> *"The word* [the gospel] *is near you; it is in your mouth and in your heart," that is, the word of faith we are proclaiming: That if you*

*confess with your mouth, "Jesus is Lord,"
and believe in your heart that God raised
him from the dead, you will be saved.*
(Romans 10:8–9 NIV)

God has an answer for your problem. He offers you salvation, deliverance, healing, and peace. There are just two conditions. First, you have to believe in your heart the record of the gospel that God raised Jesus from the dead. Yet believing in your heart, by itself, is not enough. The gospel demands a response of faith. Therefore, you also have to confess with your mouth, "Jesus is Lord."

If you will willingly yield to the lordship of Jesus in your life, you can have peace right now.

What does it mean to confess Jesus as Lord? What it really means is, "Lord Jesus, I accept Your government in my life. I have made a mess of it by myself, and I am not capable of fully governing my life. I don't have the peace You promised. Right now, I make this decision to make You Lord of my life, without reservation. Come into my life and take full control. Govern me and give me Your peace. Amen."

16

The Word of God

The title of Jesus we will look at in this chapter is found mainly in the writings of John: *The Word of God*. To begin, let's look at the opening verse of John's gospel:

In the beginning was the Word, and the Word was with God, and the Word was God. (John 1:1 NIV)

The Total Mind and Counsel of God

Notice that in the above verse, the term *"the Word"* is used three times. The One so designated is Jesus in His eternal nature—not Jesus the son of Mary, but Jesus the Son of God, the One who was eternally, before creation, with God. The One who is Himself God, the second Person of the Godhead.

The Word became flesh and made his dwelling among us. We have seen his glory, the glory of the One and Only, who came from the Father, full of grace and truth. (John 1:14 NIV)

Again, *"the Word"* is a title of Jesus. He is the one and only Son, the eternal, begotten Son. He is not created but begotten. He is eternal, of one nature and being with the Father Himself. As such, He, the Word, became flesh—the incarnation—and lived for a while among

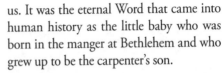

The eternal Word came into human history as the little baby who was born in the manger at Bethlehem.

us. It was the eternal Word that came into human history as the little baby who was born in the manger at Bethlehem and who grew up to be the carpenter's son.

Jesus not only came once as a baby, but Scripture makes it clear He also is coming back again in power and in glory to judge and to reign. There is a vivid picture of His future coming in the book of Revelation. Once again, in this context, He is called "*the Word of God*." John the Revelator says this:

I saw heaven standing open and there before me was a white horse, whose rider is called Faithful and True [the rider is Jesus]. *With justice he judges and makes war. His eyes are like blazing fire, and on his head are many crowns. He has a name written on him that no one knows but he himself. He is dressed in a robe dipped in blood, and his name is the Word of God.*
(Revelation 19:11–13 NIV)

So, there again is "*the Word*" in His glorious majesty, coming to judge and to reign, wearing many kingly crowns, dressed in a robe dipped in blood (which speaks of His sacrifice of Himself on the cross), and His name is the Word of God. The Greek word translated "*Word*" is *logos*. It is a word that is used quite frequently today in various contexts. We need to understand a little about this term.

A friend of mine is a Greek Orthodox priest whose native language is Greek. (I also studied Greek myself from the time I was ten years old.) This friend gave me a lecture on the meaning of the word *logos* that I never forgot. He said, "*Logos* isn't just a spoken word. *Logos* means 'mind,' it means 'counsel,' it means a whole understanding."

That is what Jesus is. He is not just a spoken word, but He is the total mind and counsel of God. Everything God knows, everything God wants to say, everything God wants to do is all wrapped up in Jesus, the Word of God.

The Full and Final Revelation of God

We need to recognize the unique function of words. Words are the supreme medium of communication. Without words, we can use signs and gestures, express certain basic feelings, and communicate certain basic needs. But without words, we also can never communicate to one another the true contents of our hearts. We cannot really say what we want to say. We cannot express deep and intimate feelings and longings, nor talk about what is interesting, stimulating, enriching, and really worth talking about.

Jesus is the Word of God. God reveals Himself in many ways: in creation, in history, and so forth. But when God really wants to say what is in His heart, He has only one way to say it: He says it in Jesus. Jesus is the full and ultimate revelation of God. Only He knows God totally.

Let's look at the description in Hebrews of who Jesus is in His eternal nature.

> *In the past God spoke to our forefathers through the prophets at many times and in various ways, but in these last days he has spoken to us by his Son....* (Hebrews 1:1–2 NIV)

The word "*last*" is significant. Jesus is the last word of God. The prophets had much to say, but when God wanted to say everything, to sum it all up, He sent His Son. This is how the Son is described:

> *...whom he appointed heir of all things, and through whom he made the universe. The Son is the radiance of God's glory and the exact representation of his being, sustaining all things by his powerful word. After he had provided purification for sins, he sat down at the right hand of the Majesty in heaven.* (verses 2–3 NIV)

Jesus is the Word of God—the full, complete revelation and unfolding of all that God is, of all that God wants to say. Let me emphasize that without revelation, man cannot know God.

At one time, I was a professional philosopher, a teacher of philosophy. I studied many philosophical systems in which philosophers tried by mere natural reasoning to arrive at an understanding of whether there is a God and, if so, what God is like. I discovered that each one of them came to a different conclusion.

What that showed me is that mere reasoning and human intelligence cannot give us a true or accurate picture of God. We are dependent on God's own sovereign revelation of Himself if we are to know who God is and what He is like. It pleased God to give us this total revelation of Himself in the Person of His Son, the Word made flesh, the One in whom God has said all He has to say. Jesus is that revelation of God, the Word of God. He is the One who shows us what God is really like. The One who opens up the very heart, nature, and being of God. The One who reveals to us the mercy of God, the faithfulness of God, and the wisdom of God. The One who gives us a true picture of God.

Jesus Reveals What God the Father Is Like

It is so pathetic to see people with false pictures of God. When I was in Egypt, I saw the remains and the relics of a pharaoh's empire. And I was just shocked by the different pictures they had of God, some extremely debased and horrible. Two of their main gods were represented by the cobra and the vulture. Another god was the jackal. Can you imagine picturing God like that?

It is Jesus who tells us and shows us what God the Father is really like.

The most important conclusion of Jesus as God's last word is that He is the full and final revelation. If we reject that revelation, we cannot expect to hear from God in any other way, for there is no other way. Jesus said, "*I am **the** way…; no one comes to the Father, but through Me*" (John 14:6, emphasis added). You cannot reject Jesus and come to the Father.

Believe in Him and receive Him by asking Him to come into your life. Open your heart and mind to Him today. He will show you the real nature of God the Father. You won't be groping or wondering. You will have a clear understanding, an ever increasing and brighter revelation of the true nature and Person of God.

May God help you to receive Him today if you have never done so before. If you have received Him, I pray that you will continue to be receptive to Him and remain open to His revelation of the Father.

You cannot reject Jesus and come to the Father.

17

The Lamb of God

John the Baptist was sent before Jesus as His forerunner to prepare the way before Him. Then, the time came for John to introduce Jesus publicly to Israel. Let's look at this account in the gospel of John:

> *The next day John saw Jesus coming toward him and said, "Look, the Lamb of God, who takes away the sin of the world! This is the one I meant when I said, 'A man who comes after me has surpassed me because he was before me.' I myself did not know him, but the reason I came baptizing with water was that he might be revealed to Israel."* (John 1:29–31 NIV)

John the Baptist came to prepare the Israelites for the kingdom of God and to reveal the Messiah to them. When he gave them this revelation, the statement he used was, "Look, the Lamb of God, who takes away the sin of the world!"

Three Scriptural Associations in the Lamb

What does this particular title, *The Lamb of God*, tell us about Jesus? I suggest to you that there are three main associations in Scripture in regard to a lamb. Remember that all Israel was very familiar with this animal. It has played a unique part in their history from the time of their exodus from Egypt onward. So, there was not a single Israelite listening to John for whom the word *lamb* did not have a very special meaning.

Here are the three associations I see in the lamb:

First, the lamb is a picture of *meekness*. This is not an animal that fights. It does not have talons, claws, or fangs. It is a meek animal.

Second, a lamb is a picture of *purity*. If you go out in the fields in the springtime and look at the newborn lambs, they look so clean and white and fluffy. There is something about them that makes you want to just pick them up and cuddle them.

The lamb was God's appointed sacrifice to provide redemption and protection.

Third—and this is the most important of all—in the history of Israel, the lamb was *God's appointed sacrifice to provide redemption and protection*. For the Jews, the lamb was particularly associated with one of their most solemn and important religious commemorations, one that is still celebrated all over the world today by Jewish people: the Passover.

The Passover Lamb

The original account of how God intended Israel to celebrate the Passover, as given to the Israelites through Moses, is recorded in Exodus 12. You will see that the whole Passover, as ordained by God, centered around a lamb; without a lamb, there could be no Passover:

> *Then Moses summoned all the elders of Israel and said to them, "Go at once and select the animals for your families and slaughter the Passover lamb. Take a bunch of hyssop, dip it into the blood in the basin and put some of the blood on the top and on both sides of the doorframe. Not one of you shall go out the door of his house until morning. When the LORD goes through the land to strike down the Egyptians, he will see the blood on the top and sides of*

the doorframe and will pass over that doorway, and he will not permit the destroyer to enter your houses and strike you down."
(Exodus 12:21–23 NIV)

The entire deliverance of Israel from judgment and wrath depended on the lamb and its blood. They had to apply the blood upon the outsides of the houses in which they lived.

That word *"Passover"* is interesting. In Hebrew, it is *Pesach*. Many years ago, I was studying Hebrew at the Hebrew University in Jerusalem. While my wife, Ruth, and I were there, we read the account of a hurricane that was approaching our home in southeast Florida. Of course, we were praying earnestly, and God did a marvelous thing. Just at the last moment, when the hurricane was about one hour away, without any obvious reason, it changed course and passed by our home city without doing any damage.

Interestingly enough, in our class, we were studying a Hebrew newspaper that reported this incident, and when it spoke about the hurricane "passing by," it used the word *frumpesach*, whose root word is the same as the word for Passover. The other students in the class asked, "What does that mean?" And I said, "You ought to know what that means. That is the word for Passover."

This was such a vivid illustration to me of what the Passover means: it means that the hurricane of God's wrath and judgment was deflected. It passed by because of the blood of the Passover lamb.

A Type Fulfilled in Jesus

The Passover lamb was a type that was fulfilled in Jesus, the Lamb of God. First, we have this prophetic picture in Isaiah:

He was oppressed and afflicted, yet he did not open his mouth; he was led like a lamb to the slaughter [a picture of meekness], *and as a sheep before her shearers is silent, so he did not open his mouth.*
(Isaiah 53:7 NIV)

A good many years ago, I worked on a farm with sheep, and I noticed how amazingly accurate that Scripture is. When you take a sheep to be shorn, it will bleat loudly all the way until you actually pick up the shears and start clipping off the wool. At that moment, the sheep becomes absolutely silent. How accurate the Scripture is when it says, *"As a sheep before her shearers is silent, so he* [Jesus] *did not open his mouth."*

The fulfillment of this verse is recorded in the Gospels. Let us look in Mark's gospel at the account of Jesus before the Sanhedrin:

> *The chief priests and the whole Sanhedrin were looking for evidence against Jesus so that they could put him to death, but they did not find any. Many testified falsely against him, but their statements did not agree....Then the high priest stood up before them and asked Jesus, "Are you not going to answer? What is this testimony that these men are bringing against you?" But Jesus remained silent and gave no answer.*
> (Mark 14:55–56, 60–61 NIV)

There Jesus was, the sheep before the shearers, absolutely silent. The same thing happened before Pilate, the Roman governor:

> *The chief priests accused him of many things. So again Pilate asked him, "Aren't you going to answer? See how many things they are accusing you of." But Jesus still made no reply, and Pilate was amazed.*
> (Mark 15:3–5 NIV)

The Lamb of God provides eternal salvation for all who believe in His atoning death and receive Him as their Savior.

The Blood of the Lamb

The blood of the Passover lamb saved (redeemed) the Israelites from being destroyed (see Exodus 12:21–23), so they could be brought out of Egypt and be led to the Promised Land. But the blood of Jesus, the Lamb of God, provides *eternal* salvation for all who believe in His atoning death and who receive Him as their Savior

and Lord. This is stated clearly many times in the New Testament. For instance, it says in Hebrews,

> *When Christ came as high priest of the good things that are already here, he went through the greater and more perfect tabernacle that is not man-made, that is to say, not a part of this creation. He did not enter by means of the blood of goats and calves; but he entered the Most Holy Place once for all by his own blood, having obtained eternal redemption.*
> (Hebrews 9:11–12 NIV)

The blood of Jesus obtained eternal redemption for every believer.

> *For you know that it was not with perishable things such as silver or gold that you were redeemed from the empty way of life handed down to you from your forefathers, but with the precious blood of Christ, a lamb without blemish or defect.*
> (1 Peter 1:18–19 NIV)

It took the blood of Jesus, the Lamb of God—God's sinless, eternal Son—to provide eternal redemption. The blood of the Passover lamb was a type, a figure. It provided temporary redemption. It had to be renewed every year. But when Jesus shed His blood and entered into the holiest, that was once and for all. It never had to be repeated. He had obtained eternal redemption.

A Pattern for Us

Finally, we see that the nature of Jesus as the Lamb of God provides an example and a pattern that we need to learn to follow in our lives.

> *To this you were called, because Christ suffered for you, leaving you an example, that you should follow in his steps. "He committed no sin, and no deceit was found in his mouth." When they hurled their insults at him, he did not retaliate; when he suffered, he made no threats.* (1 Peter 2:21–23 NIV)

There Jesus was—the spotless, meek Lamb of God—standing before His accusers, offering no defense, no retaliation. That is the lamb nature in the Son of God.

God makes it very clear that we who are believers and followers of Jesus have to reproduce that lamb nature. He set us an example to follow: "*He committed no sin, and no deceit was found in his mouth.' When they hurled their insults at him, he did not retaliate; when he suffered, he made no threats.*" That is part of the nature of Jesus that God wants to work in each one of us.

18

The Lion of the Tribe of Judah

For this chapter, I have deliberately chosen a title that is in the strongest possible contrast to that of the previous chapter. What two animals could be in greater contrast to each other than a lamb and a lion? Yet Jesus combines the qualities of both within Himself. This fact illustrates a principle that I have already stated: each title of Jesus reveals some important aspect of His wonderful, many-sided nature.

"The Lion Has Triumphed"

The title *The Lion of the Tribe of Judah* is found in the book of Revelation. In chapter 5, John the Revelator described a vision he was permitted to witness in heaven. It is a scene of majesty and grandeur, and it portrays the very throne of God. This is what John saw in the place where God's throne stands:

> *Then I saw in the right hand of him who sat on the throne a scroll with writing on both sides and sealed with seven seals. And I saw a mighty angel proclaiming in a loud voice, "Who is worthy to break the seals and open the scroll?" But no one in heaven or on earth or under the earth could open the scroll or even look inside it.* (Revelation 5:1–3 NIV)

This scroll was the revelation of what lay ahead in human history and destiny up to the close of the present age. Of course, John longed to know what God was seeking to reveal. But the lesson here is that strength did not prevail to open the scroll. Though it was a mighty angel who proclaimed in a loud voice, no one responded, no one was worthy. So John was deeply grieved, and he wrote,

> *I wept and wept because no one was found who was worthy to open the scroll or look inside. Then one of the elders said to me, "Do not weep! See, the Lion of the tribe of Judah, the Root of David, has triumphed. He is able to open the scroll and its seven seals."* (Revelation 5:4–5 NIV)

"*The Lion of the tribe of Judah*" is Jesus. He is also "*the Root of David,*" the one out of whom David received his kingly authority.

At this point, John looked toward the throne expecting to see this lion, but he saw something very different.

> *Then I saw a Lamb, looking as if it had been slain, standing in the center of the throne, encircled by the four living creatures and the elders. He had seven horns and seven eyes, which are the seven spirits of God sent out into all the earth.* (verse 6 NIV)

A Great Paradox

Can you see the deliberate paradox? Jesus was proclaimed as the Lion, but when John looked, he saw a slain Lamb. John continued,

> *He [the Lamb] came and took the scroll from the right hand of him who sat on the throne. And when he had taken it, the four living creatures and the twenty-four elders fell down before the Lamb. Each one had a harp and they were holding golden bowls full of incense, which are the prayers of the saints. And they sang a new song: "You are worthy to take the scroll and to open its seals, because you were slain, and with your blood you purchased men for God from every tribe and language and people and nation."* (Revelation 5:7–9 NIV)

Remember in the last chapter about the Lamb of God, I pointed out that it was through one Lamb's blood that redemption was provided. The Passover lamb provided temporary redemption. But Jesus, the eternal Son of God, the Lamb of God, provides eternal redemption through His blood.

So you see again the deliberate paradox: the Lamb has become the Lion. Also, in connection with the title *"the Lion of the tribe of Judah"* (verse 5), notice that this is an eternal picture and an eternal title of Jesus. It is Jesus exalted forever at God's right hand. He is still called the Lion of the tribe of Judah. That designation is very significant.

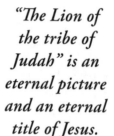

"The Lion of the tribe of Judah" is an eternal picture and an eternal title of Jesus.

Jesus did not identify Himself only temporarily with humanity through the incarnation. He became man forever without losing His identity as God. Furthermore, His identity with the Jewish people was not temporary. He is forever the Lion of the tribe of Judah. He has a special connection with the Jewish people.

Characteristics of the Lion

Let's look now at some characteristics associated with the lion, as depicted in the book of Proverbs.

First, the lion inspires fear: *"A king's rage is like the roar of a lion, but his favor is like dew on the grass"* (Proverbs 19:12 NIV). Jesus is the Lion whose roar inspires fear. But, thank God, His favor *"is like dew on the grass."*

Second, the Lion is pictured as fearless: *"The wicked man flees though no one pursues, but the righteous are as bold as a lion"* (Proverbs 28:1 NIV). Boldness is a part of the nature of a lion.

Third, the lion is pictured as irresistible. In Proverbs 30, four impressive creatures are particularly stated and described. The first and most impressive is the lion.

There are three things that are stately in their stride, four that move with stately bearing: a lion, mighty among beasts, who retreats before nothing; a strutting rooster, a he-goat, and a king with his army around him. (Proverbs 30:29–31 NIV)

Notice that the "*lion, mighty among beasts,...retreats before nothing.*" Jesus is the irresistible, all-conquering Lion of the tribe of Judah. The Lion possesses great strength. He is fearful. He is awe-inspiring. We could be frightened of Him. But we must understand this beautiful truth: if we receive the Lamb, we don't need to fear the Lion.

An Eternal Principle

An eternal principle is represented in the composite picture of Jesus as the Lamb and the Lion: in God's economy, meekness is the appointed way to true strength. That principle is very different from the human viewpoint. God says, in effect, "If you want to become strong, you have to become weak. If you want to be exalted, you have to become lowly."

Paul wrote in 1 Corinthians about the kind of people whom God receives as His own:

Where is the wise man? Where is the scholar? Where is the philosopher of this age? Has not God made foolish the wisdom of the world? For since in the wisdom of God the world through its wisdom did not know him, God was pleased through the foolishness of what was preached to save those who believe. Jews demand miraculous signs and Greeks look for wisdom, but we preach Christ crucified: a stumbling block to Jews and foolishness to Gentiles, but to those whom God has called, both Jews and Greeks, Christ the power of God and the wisdom of God. (1 Corinthians 1:20–24 NIV)

Here is the application:

For the foolishness of God is wiser than man's wisdom, and the weakness of God is stronger than man's strength. (verse 25 NIV)

All of this is represented in the Lamb. It seems foolish to the natural mind, but the ultimate revelation of God's wisdom and of God's strength is contained in the Lamb.

Note what Paul said about his own experiences:

To keep me from becoming conceited because of these surpassingly great revelations, there was given me a thorn in my flesh, a messenger of Satan, to torment me. Three times I pleaded with the Lord to take it away from me. But he said to me, "My grace is sufficient for you, for my power is made perfect in weakness." Therefore I will boast all the more gladly about my weaknesses, so that Christ's power may rest on me. That is why, for Christ's sake, I delight in weaknesses, in insults, in hardships, in persecutions, in difficulties. For when I am weak, then I am strong.
(2 Corinthians 12:7–10 NIV)

That is the lesson of the Lamb and the Lion. If you want to be strong with God's strength, you have to be weak in your own strength. If you want to be exalted, you have to be humbled. The way to become a lion is to start as a lamb. That is the wisdom of God, but it is foolishness to men. It is the strength of God, but it is considered weakness in man's eyes.

If you want to be strong with God's strength, you have to be weak in your own strength. That is the wisdom of God.

Thank God, Jesus proved, once and for all, that the foolishness of God is wiser than man's wisdom and the weakness of God is stronger than man's strength. It is all summed up in the Lamb who became the Lion.

19

Savior

The title I am presenting in this chapter is perhaps the simplest and yet the most wonderful of all the titles of Jesus. It is *Savior*.

Salvation Is in a Person

The Revelation Given by the Angel

The title *Savior* was given by revelation through an angel to Joseph when Mary was espoused to him but they were not yet married. The angel said,

> *Joseph son of David, do not be afraid to take Mary home as your wife, because what is conceived in her is from the Holy Spirit. She will give birth to a son, and you are to give him the name Jesus, because he will save his people from their sins.*
> (Matthew 1:20–21 NIV)

The angel's statement, "*You are to give him the name Jesus, because he will save his people from their sins,*" indicates that the name *Jesus* means "Savior," yet we also know this from the origin of the word. In Hebrew, the name *Jesus* is *Yeshua*, which is another form of a familiar name from the Old Testament, *Yehoshua*, or Joshua. The name *Yeshua*, or *Yehoshua*, means "salvation of the Lord."

It is important to see that this name was given by God Himself directly through the angel, and that it was given before Jesus' birth. It was the revelation of why God sent Jesus. He sent Him to save His people from their sins.

Let us consider for a moment the role of Joshua in the Old Testament. God brought the Israelites out of Egypt under their great leader, Moses. But Moses was not able to bring Israel into the Promised Land. It required the rising up of a new leader, Joshua, whose name means "salvation." That, I think, is a picture of what Jesus does for us in the new covenant. He is the leader who alone can bring us into the land of God's promises—the "land of salvation."

> *Salvation is in a person, not merely in religion, commandments, or rituals.*

Regarding the giving of this name and its application, it is very important to see that salvation is in a person, not merely in religion, commandments, or rituals. All those may be good, but, in themselves, they are insufficient to provide salvation. Salvation takes a Person.

The Testimony of God's Servant Simeon

This truth is brought out again in the latter part of the story of the baby Jesus. When His parents took Him to the temple to offer the appropriate sacrifices required by the Law, they encountered an old man, Simeon. Directed by the Holy Spirit, Simeon took up the infant Jesus in his arms and prayed a beautiful prayer in which he said these words to God: *"For my eyes have seen your salvation"* (Luke 2:30 NIV).

What was *"your salvation"*? It was that little infant in his arms. But in that little infant, Jesus—in that Person—was God's salvation.

Jesus' Statement to Zacchaeus

Later, in the public ministry of Jesus, there came a time when He invited Himself to the house of a tax collector named Zacchaeus.

Everybody thought that Zacchaeus was not good enough to have Jesus come to his house, and they began to murmur. But after Jesus had entered the house, He said to Zacchaeus,

> *Today salvation has come to this house, because this man, too, is a son of Abraham. For the Son of Man came to seek and to save what was lost.* (Luke 19:9–10 NIV)

How did salvation come to the house of Zacchaeus? Salvation came in the Person of Jesus. When Jesus came into that house, welcomed and received by Zacchaeus, then salvation entered the house.

God's salvation is not just in law or religion; it is in a Person. We have to know the Person to know salvation.

The Testimony of Old Testament Prophecy

The same principle is indicated prophetically in the Old Testament. For instance, in the Psalms, we find a prayer of David that is quite remarkable. David was under much oppression; he had many enemies, and his life was in danger, so he prayed these words:

> *Contend, O LORD, with those who contend with me; fight against those who fight against me.* (Psalm 35:1 NIV)

Then, he continued,

> *Say to my soul, "I am your salvation."* (verse 3 NIV)

That is an extraordinary prayer. David did not just say, "Save me." He said, "Present Yourself to me as my salvation." God recorded that prayer of David, and a thousand years later, He answered it when He sent Jesus. Anything less than God is not enough for salvation.

Again, the salvation of Jesus was prophetically foreshown by Isaiah:

> *Then you will say on that day, "I will give thanks to Thee, O LORD; for although Thou wast angry with me, Thine anger is turned away, and Thou dost comfort me. Behold, God is my salvation, I will trust and not be afraid; for the LORD GOD*

is my strength and song, and He has become my salvation."
(Isaiah 12:1–2)

We see here the same principle. This passage represents God's person, God's child, or the people of God as under the anger of God. Then, God's anger is turned away, and He comforts. At that revelation, the explanation is, "God has become my salvation."

Bear in mind that anything less than God Himself is not sufficient for salvation. But God has provided salvation in the Person of Jesus.

Salvation in a Word

To understand the full scope of the salvation God has provided for us in Jesus, we need to look at the meaning of a particular verb that is used many times in the New Testament. In the Greek language, the verb is *sozo*. It is normally translated, "to save," but it is also translated in many other ways.

For those who do not have access to the original Greek, I want to point out that there are many places where the word *sozo*, "to save,"

> *Every time this word, sozo, is used, it means that this is part of what God has provided in Jesus the Savior.*

is used. But you would not recognize those times, because the word is translated in English as "to heal," "to cure," and in other ways. Every time this word, *sozo*, is used, it means that this is part of what God has provided in Jesus the Savior. Such is the great, all-inclusive salvation Jesus brings.

For instance, this word is used in regard to the healing of an incurable disease. A woman who had a hemorrhage, or an issue of blood, which could not be cured medically, came up behind Jesus in a crowd. In faith, she touched the border of His robe and was miraculously healed. Jesus identified her as the one who touched Him.

Jesus turned and saw her. "Take heart, daughter," he said, "your faith has healed you." And the woman was healed from that moment. (Matthew 9:22 NIV)

The Greek word translated "*healed*" is *sozo*, or "saved"—"*Your faith has* [saved] *you.*" It was not just the salvation of her soul. It was the healing of her body.

The same word is used for deliverance from mental illness and demonic oppression. In Luke 8, we read about a demoniac who had a legion of demons. When he came to Jesus, the Lord drove out the demons and healed him. Let's read the end of the account:

> *The people went out to see what had happened. When they came to Jesus, they found the man from whom the demons had gone out, sitting at Jesus' feet, dressed and in his right mind; and they were afraid. Those who had seen it told the people how the demon-possessed man had been cured.*
>
> (Luke 8:35–36 NIV)

The Greek word translated "*cured*" is *sozo*, or "saved." So we see that deliverance from mental sickness and demonic oppression is part of the salvation that is in Jesus.

The same word is also used about someone being brought back from death. Jesus went to the house of Jairus, a ruler of the synagogue whose daughter had just died. But Jesus said, "*Don't be afraid; just believe, and she will be healed*" (Luke 8:50 NIV). Again, the Greek word for "healed" is *sozo*, or "saved."

Paul also used the word in speaking of his confidence in God's power to keep him to the end of his life. He said in 2 Timothy 4:18, "*The Lord will rescue me from every evil attack and will bring me safely to his heavenly kingdom*" (NIV). In Greek, the word translated "*bring me safely*" is *sozo*: "*The Lord…will* [save me] *to his heavenly kingdom.*" So, salvation means God's ongoing preservation of His people, as well.

Salvation is God's total provision for every need of humanity, in time and for eternity.

20

Christ, or Messiah

As we put these titles together and meditate on the significance of each, we see Jesus Himself in a much clearer and fuller way. I will now introduce another title that is simple and meaningful: *Christ*.

Christ and Messiah Have Identical Meanings

Some people do not realize that *Christ* is a title. Let me just take a moment to explain to you the background of the word. It is taken from the New Testament Greek word *christos*, meaning, very simply and definitely, "anointed." It actually implies being anointed with oil.

Christos, in turn, is a representation of a word already familiar in the Old Testament in Hebrew. The Hebrew word is *mashiach*, which means exactly the same thing: "anointed." In English, we have changed it into *Messiah*.

So, the titles *Christ* in the New Testament and *Messiah* in the Old Testament mean one and the same thing: "Anointed One." Furthermore, they refer to one and

> *The titles*
> *Christ in the*
> *New Testament*
> *and Messiah*
> *in the Old*
> *Testament mean*
> *"Anointed One."*

the same Person, Jesus. It is remarkable that many Christians do not realize that *Christ* is the same as *Messiah*. It is equally remarkable how many Jewish people do not realize that *Messiah* is the same as *Christ*. But whichever title we use, we mean the Anointed One.

Let's look at the message given by the angel to the shepherds at the time of Jesus' birth. The angel said,

> *Today in the town of David a Savior has been born to you; he is*
> *Christ the Lord.*　　　　　　　　　　　　(Luke 2:11 NIV)

So, the Savior is the Christ—the Anointed One. This was the fulfillment of God's long-standing promise to Israel that He would one day send them an Anointed One who would be two things: a deliverer and a king. This was a familiar concept to them, as we will see in the following examples.

Anointed to Deliver and Rule

In the book of Judges, God sent men of His choosing who became deliverers and ruled Israel for a while. Each one of those judges owed his ability to deliver Israel to the anointing of the Holy Spirit upon him. After that, when God gave Israel kings, the kings were set apart by the ceremony of anointing with oil. This was true of Israel's first king, Saul.

> *Then Samuel took a flask of oil and poured it on Saul's head and*
> *kissed him, saying, "Has not the LORD anointed you leader over*
> *his inheritance?"*　　　　　　　　　　　(1 Samuel 10:1 NIV)

To be leader over God's inheritance, a man had to be anointed with oil. The oil, of course, is a picture, or type, of the Holy Spirit.

This fact is brought out even more clearly in the case of Israel's second king, David. God sent Samuel to the house of Jesse to anoint the king, and the appointed king was the youngest son, David. In 1 Samuel 16:13, we read,

> *So Samuel took the horn of oil and anointed him* [David] *in the*
> *presence of his brothers, and from that day on the Spirit of the*
> *LORD came upon David in power.*　　　　　　　　　　　(NIV)

Here we see David being set apart by the anointing with oil to be the deliverer and king for Israel. The inner meaning of the anointing is brought out in the second part of the verse: "*from that day on the Spirit of the Lord came upon David in power.*" In keeping with this, the Christ, or the Messiah, is the One anointed with the power of the Holy Spirit to be a Deliverer and a Ruler.

The Greatest Deliverer and King

That there was to be a greater Deliverer and Ruler to come, even greater than David, is stated in various places in the Old Testament, including the eleventh chapter of Isaiah:

Then a shoot will spring from the stem of Jesse, and a branch from his roots will bear fruit. [It promises that this Deliverer and King will come from the line of David.] *And the Spirit of the LORD will rest on Him, the spirit of wisdom and understanding, the spirit of counsel and strength, the spirit of knowledge and the fear of the LORD. And He will delight in the fear of the LORD, and He will not judge by what His eyes see, nor make a decision by what His ears hear; but with righteousness He will judge the poor, and decide with fairness for the afflicted of the earth; and He will strike the earth with the rod of His mouth, and with the breath of His lips He will slay the wicked.*

(Isaiah 11:1–4)

Here is God's righteous King who is absolutely fair, impartial, and discerning in all His judgments and in the administration of His kingdom.

The same promise is given again later in Isaiah, where the Messiah is portrayed. Speaking in the first person, He says,

The Spirit of the Lord GOD is upon me, because the LORD has anointed me to bring good news to the afflicted; He has sent me to bind up the brokenhearted, to proclaim liberty to captives, and freedom to prisoners. (Isaiah 61:1)

Here, again, it all depends on the anointing of the Holy Spirit. The One who is thus anointed by the Holy Spirit is the One who

---

All God's promises about the Anointed Messiah found their fulfillment in Jesus of Nazareth.

---

is sent by God with a message of mercy, love, grace, and healing power, to bind up the brokenhearted and to proclaim liberty to captives and freedom to prisoners. That was the promise of the Messiah, the Christ, the Anointed One. All God's promises about the Anointed Messiah, the Christ, the Deliverer, and the King found their fulfillment in Jesus of Nazareth.

Jesus Is Anointed by the Holy Spirit

Let's look at three passages from the fourth chapter of Luke's gospel that bring out this fact. When the Holy Spirit came upon Jesus at the river Jordan, Jesus became the Anointed, the Messiah. From eternity, He was destined to be the Anointed, but at a certain point in history, when the Holy Spirit came upon Him, He became the Anointed in actual effect. This is the description of what happened to Jesus after His baptism in the Jordan by John the Baptist.

> *Jesus, full of the Holy Spirit, returned from the Jordan and was led about by the Spirit in the wilderness.* (Luke 4:1)

Note that He was filled with the Holy Spirit and He was led by the Holy Spirit. The anointing was upon Him. Then, after His temptation in the wilderness, the Scripture says,

> *Jesus returned to Galilee in the power of the Spirit; and news about Him spread through all the surrounding district.* (Luke 4:14)

We see that, in verse 1, He was filled with the Holy Spirit and led by the Spirit, and that, by verse 14, He was empowered by the Spirit. He was truly the *mashiach*, the Messiah; the *christos*, the Anointed.

Next, we read how Jesus declared that He was the fulfillment of God's promise. He entered the synagogue in Nazareth and read Isaiah 61:1, which we already looked at, and applied it to Himself:

And the book of the prophet Isaiah was handed to Him [Jesus]. *And He opened the book, and found the place where it was written, "The Spirit of the Lord is upon Me, because He anointed Me to preach the gospel to the poor. He has sent Me to proclaim release to the captives, and recovery of sight to the blind, to set free those who are downtrodden, to proclaim the favorable year of the Lord."* (Luke 4:17–18)

Then, Jesus closed the book, and in words of tremendous historical significance, He said to them, *"Today this Scripture has been fulfilled in your hearing"* (verse 21). In other words, Jesus was saying, "I am the One; I am the Anointed. The Spirit of the Lord is upon Me." And He went forth from that moment as the Deliverer, bringing release to the captives and recovery of sight to the blind, setting free those who were downtrodden, and proclaiming the gospel to the poor.

The Anointed One

This marvelous ministry of Jesus, the Anointed, the Christ, the Messiah, is summed up by Peter in one verse. As he was speaking to the household of Cornelius, Peter described what he had witnessed in the ministry of Jesus:

You know of Jesus of Nazareth, how God anointed Him with the Holy Spirit and with power, and how He went about doing good, and healing all who were oppressed by the devil; for God was with Him. (Acts 10:38)

That is a summation of the ministry of Jesus as the Messiah, the Anointed, the Christ. God anointed Him with the Holy Spirit. God was with Him. And in the power of that anointing, He went about doing good and healing all who were oppressed by the devil.

It always blesses me to see that healing is attributed to God and sickness to the devil. Also, in that verse we have all three Persons of the Godhead. God the Father anointed Jesus the Son with the Spirit, and the result was healing and deliverance for all humanity. What a blessed message—the message of the Christ.

21

The Alpha and the Omega

Jesus' title *The Alpha and the Omega* emphasizes that He proceeds out of eternity and spans all time. John the Revelator wrote about the visible return of Jesus in glory:

> *Look, he is coming with the clouds, and every eye will see him, even those who pierced him; and all the peoples of the earth will mourn because of him. So shall it be! Amen. "I am the Alpha and the Omega," says the Lord God, "who is, and who was, and who is to come, the Almighty."* (Revelation 1:7–8 NIV)

To understand the full meaning of the title *The Alpha and the Omega*, we need to familiarize ourselves a little with the Greek alphabet. While in the English alphabet, *a* is the first letter and *z* is the last, the Greek alphabet begins with the letter *alpha* and ends with the letter *omega*.

We have already seen that Jesus is the Word of God. When Jesus says, *"I am the Alpha and the Omega,"* He means that He is the complete Word of God. Everything that God has to say is summed up in Him. It also means that everything God does begins and ends with Jesus. He is the beginning and the ending.

Everything God does begins and ends with Jesus.

Where it says, "*the Lord God, 'who is, and who was, and who is to come,'*" it is the same picture. God *is* now, He *was* in the past, and He *will* be—all at once. He is the Alpha and the Omega.

The Beginning and the Culmination

This truth has a particular application to the close of the present age, because the age is going to close in Jesus. He is going to be the One who will bring this age to its close. As He was Alpha at the beginning, so He will be Omega at the end. This truth is brought out in the book of Hebrews, where the writer said,

> *In the past God spoke to our forefathers through the prophets at many times and in various ways, but in these last days he has spoken to us by his Son, whom he [God] appointed heir of all things, and through whom he made the universe.*
> (Hebrews 1:1–2 NIV)

We see from this passage that Jesus was at the beginning of creation. Through Him, God made the universe. He was Alpha. He is also the appointed heir of all things. Everything is going to be summed up and come to its culmination in Jesus.

As the Creator, He is Alpha. As the heir of all things, He is Omega. He spans all time. He proceeds out of eternity, on through time, and into eternity. He is the Eternal, the Uncreated, the Only Begotten of the Father, the Beginning and the End.

We need to understand that God has a dual relationship with time: He transcends time, but He also operates within time. God works in time, but He Himself is outside of time and before time. It is hard for the human mind to comprehend this concept, but there are beautiful pictures in Scripture that present it to us. For instance, the psalmist addressed God with these words:

> *Before the mountains were born or you brought forth the earth and the world, from everlasting to everlasting you are God.*
> (Psalm 90:2 NIV)

In a sense, there is always a present tense with God, but He is from everlasting to everlasting. He is from eternity to eternity. He comprehends all time. He is the beginning and the ending, the Alpha and the Omega.

Christ's Timelessness

Prophetically, this truth was specifically applied to the coming Messiah, the coming King, fulfilled in Jesus. For instance, Micah the prophet said of the Messiah who was to come,

But you, Bethlehem Ephrathah, though you are small among the clans of Judah, out of you will come for me one who will be ruler over Israel, whose origins are from of old, from ancient times.
(Micah 5:2 NIV)

What a clear prediction of the birth of Jesus! It was foretold that the Messiah was to come out of Bethlehem, the city of David, and that He was to be the One who was to rule for God His people Israel. Then, it says at the end, *"Whose origins are from of old, from ancient times."*

Although He was born as the babe in the stable in Bethlehem, His origin is from eternity. He is Alpha and Omega. He came into time, but He was not of time. He was from eternity; He is to eternity.

Jesus said the same about Himself. He was speaking to the Jewish people about their relationship—and His relationship—to Abraham. They were claiming that they were descendents of Abraham, in essence saying that was all that really mattered. But Jesus said something to them that absolutely startled and shook them:

"Your father Abraham rejoiced at the thought of seeing my day; he saw it and was glad." "You are not yet fifty years old," the Jews said to him, "and you have seen Abraham!" "I tell you the truth," Jesus answered, "before Abraham was born, I am!"
(John 8:56–58 NIV)

That is His eternity. That is His timelessness. Jesus was born into time, into human history, but He is from before time. He is the Alpha and the Omega, the beginning and the ending, the first and the last.

Alpha and Omega in Our Lives

The title *The Alpha and the Omega* also depicts the place of Jesus in our individual lives. It is not solely in relationship to creation and the universe that He is Alpha and Omega, but it is also the position that He occupies in the life of each one of us who believes in Him. Here is what the writer of Hebrews said:

> *Therefore, since we are surrounded by such a great cloud of witnesses, let us throw off everything that hinders and the sin that so easily entangles, and let us run with perseverance the race marked out for us. Let us fix our eyes on Jesus, the author and perfecter of our faith.* (Hebrews 12:1–2 NIV)

Jesus is the author, or the beginner (the Alpha), and the perfecter, or the completer (the Omega). As long as we keep our eyes on Jesus, we find *in* Him and *through* Him everything we need. There is nothing outside of Jesus that we need. He spans our whole need, from Alpha to Omega.

As long as we keep our eyes on Jesus, we find in Him and through Him everything we need.

The important reminder is that we must not take our eyes off Jesus. We must not think that somehow Jesus isn't able to provide all that we need and start looking in some other direction. He can. He is. He is God's whole alphabet, from Alpha to Omega.

God's Eternal Purpose

Again, in Ephesians, we see a beautiful picture of God's dealings with us in Christ:

For he [God] *chose us in him* [Christ] *before the creation of the world to be holy and blameless in his sight. In love he predestined us to be adopted as his sons through Jesus Christ, in accordance with his pleasure and will—to the praise of his glorious grace, which he has freely given us in the One he loves. In him we have redemption through his blood, the forgiveness of sins, in accordance with the riches of God's grace that he lavished on us with all wisdom and understanding. And he made known to us the mystery of his will according to his good pleasure, which he purposed in Christ, to be put into effect when the times will have reached their fulfillment—to bring all things in heaven and on earth together under one head, even Christ.* (Ephesians 1:4–10 NIV)

Before creation—before time ever began—God chose us in Christ to be His. That was His eternal purpose. Then, in time, He called us. He revealed Jesus to us. He transformed us. He made us into His children. And then, above all that, He made known to us the mystery of His ultimate purpose: "*He made known to us the mystery of his will according to his good pleasure, which he purposed in Christ, to be put into effect when the times will have reached their fulfillment.*"

When time will have run its course, God's purpose is this: "*to bring all things in heaven and on earth together under one head, even Christ.*" It all started in Christ, before time ever began. It will all end and find fulfillment and completion in Christ, after time has ended.

Christ is the Alpha and the Omega, the beginning and the ending, the first and the last. He is all that we need. He is the entire alphabet, from Alpha to Omega.

22

The Bright Morning Star

Like *The Alpha and the Omega*, the title we are going to study in this chapter is taken from the book of Revelation. At the end of the book, Jesus spoke to John the Revelator, saying,

> *I, Jesus, have sent my angel to give you this testimony for the churches. I am the Root and the Offspring of David, and the bright Morning Star.* (Revelation 22:16 NIV)

Actually, there are two titles in this verse: "*the Root and the Offspring of David*" and "*the bright Morning Star.*" If we look for a moment at *The Root and the Offspring of David*, we see that it corresponds, in a certain sense, with the title we looked at in the previous chapter, *The Alpha and the Omega*. But it has special application to David and his house. As Root, Jesus was Alpha to David's house. As Offspring, He is Omega. He is the One from whom they were initiated, but also the One in whom they will find fulfillment.

The title we want to focus on from this verse, however, is *The Bright Morning Star*. The term *morning star* is used by some to refer to the sun.

Jesus, the Radiance of the "Sun"

Jesus is called the morning star, or the sun, because of certain specific and unique features of the sun in our world. I will emphasize two of these features.

First, the sun is the sole, universal source of light and heat for the earth; therefore, it is the source of life itself. Without the sun, there can be no life in our world. It supplies everywhere both light and heat.

Second, the sun, because of the fact that it rises and sets—appears and disappears—always carries with it the promise of sunrise after darkness.

Universal Source of Light and Heat

For some Scriptures corresponding to the first application—the sun as the earth's universal source of light and heat—let us begin with Psalm 19. This psalm provides a vivid and beautiful picture of the heavenly bodies—the sun, in particular. The psalmist wrote,

> *In the heavens he* [God] *has pitched a tent for the sun, which is like a bridegroom coming forth from his pavilion, like a champion rejoicing to run his course. It rises at one end of the heavens and makes its circuit to the other; nothing is hidden from its heat.*
>
> (Psalm 19:4–6 NIV)

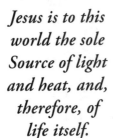

> *Jesus is to this world the sole Source of light and heat, and, therefore, of life itself.*

Isn't that description beautiful? The heavens are like the tent for the sun. These verses speak of both the beauty and the strength of the sun. It is like a bridegroom adorned in his glorious attire, and it is like a champion who runs a race in full strength.

That everything in our world derives light and heat from one unique source—the sun—is a profound scientific truth that we recognize today. That is how Jesus is to this world. He is the sole Source of light and heat, and, therefore, of life itself. He is like the bridegroom and like the strong man. He is both beautiful and glorious.

Let's look again in Hebrews 1 for further application of this truth:

> *In the past God spoke to our forefathers through the prophets at many times and in various ways, but in these last days he has spoken to us by his Son, whom he appointed heir of all things, and through whom he made the universe. The Son is the radiance of God's glory and the exact representation of his being, sustaining all things by his powerful word.* (Hebrews 1:1–3 NIV)

Of course, the word "*Son*" in that last phrase is spelled s–o–n, but the phrase "*the radiance of God's glory*" immediately reminds us of the sun, s–u–n. Jesus is the radiance of the glory of the "sun," which is God the Father. There is a parable in the reality of the sun and its light. Let me just take a moment to unfold this to you because it is so beautiful. It is a picture of the total nature of God—Father, Son, and Holy Spirit. It is represented to us by the sun, by its light, and by our experience.

The substance of the sun represents God the Father. Nobody has ever seen the substance of the sun; nobody has ever seen God the Father. The manifest brightness—the radiance of the sun—represents God the Son. The rays that convey that brightness to us, that make it possible for us to actually see that brightness, represent God the Holy Spirit. Interestingly enough, these rays are refracted in the rainbow into seven colors, the distinctive number of the Holy Spirit. That is just a little parable from nature.

By analogy, therefore, the substance of the sun is God the Father, the radiance of the glory of the sun is Jesus Christ the Son, and the rays that convey that radiance to you and me are the Holy Spirit.

Promise of Sunrise after Darkness

The second characteristic I cited about the sun, as it represents Jesus, is that it always carries with it the promise of sunrise after darkness. This spiritual reality is clearly predicted in Malachi:

> *"For behold, the day is coming, burning like an oven, and all the proud, yes, all who do wickedly will be stubble. And the day which is coming shall burn them up," says the LORD of hosts, "that will leave them neither root nor branch. But to you who fear ["revere" NIV] My name the Sun of Righteousness shall arise with healing in His wings; and you shall go out and grow fat like stall-fed calves.*   (Malachi 4:1–2 NKJV)

Scripture warns us there is coming a time of God's wrath and indignation on the wicked and the rebellious. But at the same time, in the midst of the warning, God gives us a promise of deliverance and help that comes in the Person of the *"Sun of Righteousness"*—the Lord Jesus.

Out of the midst of all the anguish, the tribulation, and the darkness, there is going to arise that Bright Morning Star, the Sun of Righteousness, with healing in its wings. It is going to bring deliverance and healing, rest and peace to those who revere, or fear, God's name.

Peter, speaking about the promise of the coming of the Lord Jesus in glory, said it requires preparation on our part. There has to be an inner preparation before the Sun of Righteousness will arise for us with healing and deliverance. That means something has to happen inside each one of us personally. It is important for us to understand this. Peter wrote,

> *We did not follow cleverly invented stories when we told you about the power and coming of our Lord Jesus Christ, but we were eyewitnesses of his majesty. For he received honor and glory from God the Father when the voice came to him from the Majestic Glory, saying, "This is my Son, whom I love; with*

him I am well pleased." We ourselves heard this voice that came from heaven when we were with him on the sacred mountain.
(2 Peter 1:16–18 NIV)

Peter was looking back in his memory to that scene on the Mount of Transfiguration when Jesus was transfigured before their eyes and they saw Him in His glory, in His majesty, and in His brightness. Then, Peter went on to say,

And we have the word of the prophets made more certain, and you will do well to pay attention to it, as to a light shining in a dark place, until the day dawns and the morning star rises in your hearts. (2 Peter 1:19 NIV)

The Morning Star rising in our hearts does not refer to Jesus' coming in power and glory to judge the universe. Instead, it refers to an inner, personal experience. It is when we have come to know Him personally and through the revelation of God's Word and the prophecies of Scripture. It is when we have come to a quiet, unshakable, inner confidence that Jesus is coming back to reign. That is when Jesus, the Sun of Righteousness, is going to rise for those who fear God's name.

> *The Morning Star rising in our hearts refers to an inner experience— when we have come to know Him personally and through the revelation of God's Word.*

Has the Morning Star Risen in You?

I wonder today if you have that inner assurance, if the return of Jesus in glory is a reality for you. Has that Morning Star risen in your heart?

Scripture says we do well to pay attention to the prophecies of the Bible. If we will fasten our minds on the Word of God, meditate on it, and let the Holy Spirit speak to us through it, He will make the future return of Jesus something very real to us, something about which we are absolutely confident. It will be like a star rising in our hearts. It will be there "*until the day dawns*," until the actual great event takes place, until the Sun of Righteousness arises out of the darkness of anguish and tribulation to give fresh light and hope to the people of this earth.

So, cultivate the awareness that Jesus is coming. Let it be a star that rises in your heart.

23

King of Kings and Lord of Lords

The last title that I have chosen is *King of kings and Lord of lords*. This title is also taken from the book of Revelation. In Revelation 17, we have a picture of the great, global, end-time conflict in which Satan and the rulers associated with him will actually be aligned in open war against God and His appointed ruler, Jesus. This is part of the description:

> *The ten horns you saw are ten kings who have not yet received a kingdom, but who for one hour will receive authority as kings along with the beast* [Antichrist]. *They have one purpose and will give their power and authority to the beast. They will make war against the Lamb* [Jesus], *but the Lamb will overcome them because he is Lord of lords and King of kings—and with him will be his called, chosen and faithful followers.*
> (Revelation 17:12–14 NIV)

It always blesses me that Jesus does not want to win the victory on His own. He wants to share it with His followers. That is just like Him—He wants to bring us in on everything, even His victory.

The Ultimate Ruler

In an earlier chapter, we saw that the Lamb is also the Lion. In the above passage, the Lamb is called *"Lord of lords and King of kings"* (Revelation 17:14 NIV). Again, there is a deliberate paradox in a Lamb that is the Lord of lords and King of kings.

This same title is used a little further on in the book of Revelation, where we have the revelation of Jesus ready to return from heaven in power and glory to judge the earth and to take over its kingdoms. John wrote,

> *I saw heaven standing open and there before me was a white horse, whose rider* [Jesus] *is called Faithful and True. With justice he judges and makes war. His eyes are like blazing fire, and on his head are many crowns.* [The many crowns represent all the kingdoms that are His by right.] *He has a name written on him that no one knows but he himself. He is dressed in a robe dipped in blood, and his name is the Word of God. The armies of heaven were following him, riding on white horses and dressed in fine linen, white and clean. Out of his mouth comes a sharp sword with which to strike down the nations. "He will rule them with an iron scepter." He treads the winepress of the fury of the wrath of God Almighty. On his robe and on his thigh he has this name written: KING OF KINGS AND LORD OF LORDS.*
> (Revelation 19:11–16 NIV)

Jesus is here presented very clearly and emphatically as the ultimate ruler of the universe. This passage depicts the establishment of His authority against all opposition.

Jesus' Path: Faithfulness, Resurrection, Rulership

Let's remind ourselves of the path by which Jesus came to this position. This, too, is revealed in the book of Revelation:

> *Grace and peace to you from him who is, and who was, and who is to come* [God the Father], *and from the seven spirits before his throne* [the Holy Spirit], *and from Jesus Christ, who is the*

faithful witness, the firstborn from the dead, and the ruler of the kings of the earth. (Revelation 1:4–5 NIV)

There is a certain sequence that we need to observe. First, Jesus was, in His humanity, *"the faithful witness,"* the One who never turned from the truth, the One who spoke the truth even about Himself, though it cost Him His life. He was the faithful witness.

> *Jesus was the One who spoke the truth, though it cost Him His life. He was the faithful witness.*

Then, because Jesus was the faithful witness, God vindicated His faithfulness and His righteousness and raised Him from the dead. So, He became *"the first-born from the dead,"* the first person ever to rise in resurrection out of death, never to die again—the "first-born" meaning that others, His believing people, were to follow Him in resurrection.

Third, as the firstborn from the dead, the head of a new creation, He is also the ruler of the new order. He is *"the ruler of the kings of the earth."*

Jesus Receives Authority from the Father

Let's look at those words once more. He is *"the faithful witness, the firstborn from the dead,"* and, therefore, *"the ruler of the kings of the earth"* (Revelation 1:5 NIV). It is important to see, also, that Jesus receives His authority from the Father. He does not wrest it for Himself. It is conferred upon Him because He has deserved it. He has merited it. He has fulfilled the conditions for it.

Paul stated this truth in some wonderful and beautiful words written to Timothy:

> *In the sight of God, who gives life to everything, and of Christ Jesus* [the Messiah Jesus], *who while testifying before Pontius Pilate made the good confession* [was the faithful witness], *I charge you to keep this command* [Timothy's ministry]

> *without spot or blame until the appearing of our Lord Jesus*
> *Christ, which God will bring about in his own time—God,*
> *the blessed and only Ruler, the King of kings and Lord of lords,*
> *who alone is immortal and who lives in unapproachable light,*
> *whom no one has seen or can see. To him be honor and might*
> *forever. Amen.*   (1 Timothy 6:13–16 NIV)

It is God the Father who will bring about the appearing—the return in glory—of the Lord Jesus Christ. And of God the Father, it says, He is "*the blessed and only Ruler.*" The King James Version uses "*Potentate,*" a tremendously powerful word. He is "*the King of kings and Lord of lords.*"

It is interesting to know the real meaning of that phrase in the original Greek: "the King of all who are kinging it and the Lord of all who are lording it." No matter what men may claim to be, no matter what power they may appropriate for themselves, God the Father is the King of all and the Lord of all. He imparted this authority to His chosen, well-beloved, and faithful Son, the Lord Jesus. And, out of the impartation of that authority, Jesus is King of kings and Lord of lords.

Ruler of the Universe

That beautiful title applied to Jesus has a very specific meaning. Kings and lords are rulers. It means that Jesus is the Ruler of all rulers, Governor over all governments. Particularly under His authority are all earthly rulers and governments. He is directly over them, and all must bow to Him.

Hence, Jesus wears on His head those "*many crowns*" (Revelation 19:12 NIV). The Greek word for "*crowns*" is *diadema*, from which we get the English word *diadem*. These are not crowns that represent victory in an athletic contest; that type of crown is identified by another word. Instead, it is the royal word, *diadem*. He has many crowns because all kings find their authority and their right to rule from Him.

God has a special message to rulers concerning Jesus. Sometimes, we do not realize that God says some things especially to rulers and leaders. Let's look at the whole of Psalm 2:

Why do the nations conspire and the peoples plot in vain? The kings of the earth take their stand and the rulers gather together against the LORD and against his Anointed One [Christ, or Messiah]. *"Let us break their chains," they say, "and throw off their fetters."* [They want to reject the Lordship of Jesus.] *The One enthroned in heaven* [God the Father] *laughs; the Lord scoffs at them. Then he rebukes them in his anger and terrifies them in his wrath, saying, "I have installed **my King** on Zion, my holy hill." I will proclaim the decree of the LORD* [the Father]: *He said to me, "You are my Son; today I have become your Father. Ask of me, and I will make the nations your inheritance, the ends of the earth your possession. You will rule them with an iron scepter; you will dash them to pieces like pottery." Therefore, you kings, be wise; be warned, you rulers of the earth. Serve the LORD with fear and rejoice with trembling. Kiss the Son, lest he be angry and you be destroyed in your way, for his wrath can flare up in a moment. Blessed are all who take refuge in him.*

(Psalm 2 NIV, emphasis added)

Of course, *"my King"* is Jesus. No matter what earth's rulers may decide, say, or attempt to do, Jesus, the appointed King, is already installed on the heavenly Zion. Remember, because He is the firstborn from the dead, He is the Ruler of the kings of the earth.

This psalm brings a special message, and a timely one for today—a message to the rulers of earth: be reconciled with God through Jesus. *"Kiss the Son,"* because if His anger flares up, He will bring judgment on you that you cannot resist.

The establishment of the kingdom of Jesus is the only solution to earth's problems and the only hope for earth's peoples. Thank God, He is the King of kings and Lord of lords. Come quickly, Lord Jesus!

The establishment of the kingdom of Jesus is the only solution to earth's problems and the only hope for earth's peoples.

About the Author

Derek Prince (1915–2003) was born in India of British parents. He was educated as a scholar of Greek and Latin at Eton College and King's College, Cambridge in England. Upon graduation he held a fellowship (equivalent to a professorship) in Ancient and Modern Philosophy at King's College. Prince also studied Hebrew, Aramaic, and modern languages at Cambridge and the Hebrew University in Jerusalem. As a student, he was a philosopher and self-proclaimed agnostic.

While in the British Medical Corps during World War II, Prince began to study the Bible as a philosophical work. Converted through a powerful encounter with Jesus Christ, he was baptized in the Holy Spirit a few days later. Out of this encounter, he formed two conclusions: first, that Jesus Christ is alive; second, that the Bible is a true, relevant, up-to-date book. These conclusions altered the whole course of his life, which he then devoted to studying and teaching the Bible as the Word of God.

Discharged from the army in Jerusalem in 1945, he married Lydia Christensen, founder of a children's home there. Upon their marriage, he immediately became father to Lydia's eight adopted daughters—six Jewish, one Palestinian Arab, and one English. Together, the family saw the rebirth of the state of Israel in 1948. In the late 1950s, they adopted another daughter while Prince was serving as principal of a teacher training college in Kenya.

In 1963, the Princes immigrated to the United States and pastored a church in Seattle. In 1973, Prince became one of the founders of Intercessors for America. His book *Shaping History through Prayer and Fasting* has awakened Christians around the world to their responsibility to pray for their governments. Many consider underground translations of the book as instrumental in the fall of communist regimes in the USSR, East Germany, and Czechoslovakia.

Lydia Prince died in 1975, and Prince married Ruth Baker (a single mother to three adopted children) in 1978. He met his second wife, like his first wife, while she was serving the Lord in Jerusalem. Ruth died in December 1998 in Jerusalem, where they had lived since 1981.

Until a few years before his own death in 2003 at the age of eighty-eight, Prince persisted in the ministry God had called him to as he traveled the world, imparting God's revealed truth, praying for the sick and afflicted, and sharing his prophetic insights into world events in the light of Scripture. Internationally recognized as a Bible scholar and spiritual patriarch, Derek Prince established a teaching ministry that spanned six continents and more than sixty years. He is the author of more than fifty books, six hundred audio teachings, and one hundred video teachings, many of which have been translated and published in more than one hundred languages. He pioneered teaching on such groundbreaking themes as generational curses, the biblical significance of Israel, and demonology/spiritual warfare.

Prince's radio program, which began in 1979, has been translated into more than a dozen languages and continues to touch lives. Derek's main gift of explaining the Bible and its teaching in a clear and simple way has helped build a foundation of faith in millions of lives. His nondenominational, nonsectarian approach has made his teaching equally relevant and helpful to people from all racial and religious backgrounds, and his teaching is estimated to have reached more than half the globe.

In 2002, he said, "It is my desire—and I believe the Lord's desire—that this ministry continue the work, which God began through me over sixty years ago, until Jesus returns."

Derek Prince Ministries persists in reaching out to believers in over 140 countries with Derek's teaching, fulfilling the mandate to keep on "until Jesus returns." This is effected through the outreaches of more than thirty Derek Prince offices around the world, including primary work in Australia, Canada, China, France, Germany, the Netherlands, New Zealand, Norway, Russia, South Africa, Switzerland, the United Kingdom, and the United States. For current information about these and other worldwide locations, visit www.derekprince.com.

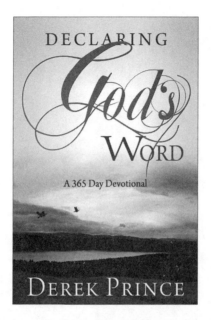

Declaring God's Word: A 365-Day Devotional
Derek Prince

According to Scripture, Satan can be defeated if believers will stand on God's Word and testify to what it says about the mighty and powerful blood of Jesus—blood that cleanses us from sin and makes us righteous. For the first time, acclaimed Bible teacher Derek Prince will lead you to power and victory in this yearlong daily devotional. By *Declaring God's Word*, you will become steeped in the Scriptures and overcome satanic oppression and attacks. Begin each new day by confessing the truth of God's Word, and you will experience the love, power, and wisdom of God all year long.

ISBN: 978-1-60374-067-8 ✦ Trade ✦ 432 pages

WHITAKER
HOUSE

Gateway to God's Blessing
Derek Prince

The Bible says that the fear of the Lord is the *"beginning of wisdom"* (Psalm 111:10) and the *"beginning of knowledge"* (Proverbs 1:7). Proverbs 14:27 even calls it a *"fountain of life"*! But do people really understand what is meant by *"the fear of the LORD"*? Drastically different from the frightful trembling we feel in response to a threatening person or dangerous situation, the fear of the Lord is a deep sense of reverence and awe of the One who created us, loves us, and saved us. With comforting words of instruction, Bible scholar Derek Prince explains how to gain wisdom, peace, and confidence that are rooted in the fear of the Lord.

ISBN: 978-1-60374-052-4 • Trade • 176 pages

WHITAKER HOUSE

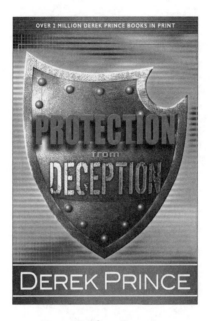

Protection from Deception
Derek Prince

According to Scripture, supernatural signs and wonders will multiply as we approach the end times. God isn't the only one with a plan, however—Satan is plotting to deceive believers with supernatural signs and wonders of his own. With relentless deceptions, the devil tries to keep us from the divine love and protection of God. But what can we do? In *Protection from Deception*, renowned Bible scholar Derek Prince will equip you to test the source of supernatural signs and wonders, discern truth from falsehood, distinguish between the Holy Spirit and counterfeit spirits, and break free from the strongholds of Satan. You, too, can uncover the enemy's strategies, effectively engage in spiritual battles—and WIN!

ISBN: 978-0-88368-230-2 • Trade • 240 pages

WHITAKER
HOUSE

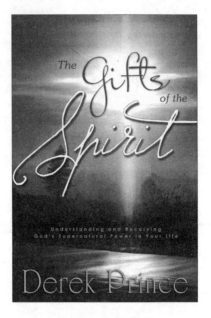

The Gifts of the Spirit
Derek Prince

Every believer has been given at least one supernatural gift of the Holy Spirit. Do you know which you have and how to operate in it? Internationally renowned Bible teacher Derek Prince explains how to stir up the gift within you in order to minister to others. One of our greatest necessities in the church today is to demonstrate through the power of the Spirit that Jesus is alive and that His gospel is true. The world needs to see the manifestation of the presence of God. Believers need the ministry of the body of Christ through spiritual gifts. *The Gifts of the Spirit* reveals how we can fulfill both of these needs—*practically* and *powerfully*.

ISBN: 978-0-88368-291-3 • Trade • 256 pages

WHITAKER
HOUSE